# Arthur Rackham

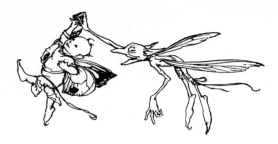

*'Imagination is always the ruling and divine power, and the rest of man is only the instrument which it sounds, or the tablet on which it writes.'*

*(John Ruskin)*

# Arthur Rackham

## FRED GETTINGS

Macmillan Publishing Co., Inc.
New York

*For my daughter Tiffany*

Macmillan Publishing Co., Inc.
866 Third Avenue, New York, N.Y. 10022

**Library of Congress Cataloging in Publication Data**

Gettings, Fred.
  Arthur Rackham.

    1. Rackham, Arthur, 1867–1939.  I. Rackham, Arthur, 1867–1939.  II. Title.
NC242.R3G47  1976      741.9'42     75-21767
ISBN 0-02-543080-7

First published in Great Britain in 1975 by Studio Vista
First American Edition 1976

Printed in Great Britain

# CONTENTS

ACKNOWLEDGEMENTS . . . . . . . . . 6

MAINLY BIOGRAPHICAL . . . . . . . . 8

EARLY ARTISTIC INFLUENCES . . . . . . . 17

TECHNIQUE AND STYLE . . . . . . . . 35

RACKHAM'S IMAGINATION . . . . . . . 77

RACKHAM'S BEST BOOK ILLUSTRATIONS 1.
    From *Two Old Ladies* to de luxe *Peter Pan* . . . . 98

RACKHAM'S BEST BOOK ILLUSTRATIONS 2.
    From the new *Alice* to the new *Toad* . . . . . 114

APPENDIX A
    Bibliography of first editions for which Rackham provided
    illustrations . . . . . . . . . . 170

APPENDIX B
    Rackham's early magazine illustrations which appeared in later books   183

APPENDIX C
    The AR monogram on the illustrations to *A Dog's Mission* and
    *The Ferryman's Boy* . . . . . . . . 188

APPENDIX D
    The errors in Martin Hardie's *Water-colour Painting in Britain*
    (Vol III *The Victorian Period*) in so far as they touch upon
    Arthur Rackham . . . . . . . . 189

APPENDIX E
    Rackham's original drawings and paintings in public collections . 190

SELECTED BIBLIOGRAPHY . . . . . . . 191

INDEX . . . . . . . . . . . 192

# ACKNOWLEDGEMENTS

Whilst most books are conveniently ascribed to one man, a truism of authorship is that rarely one man writes a book alone. There are always all those others who, sometimes with words, but more usually with nods and winks, and even with cups of tea, contribute as definitively to the book as the author himself. This book is no exception, and an accurate acknowledgement list would read as extensively as a decade's *Who's Who*, though perhaps with names a little less exclusive. I shall therefore restrict myself, and mention only the names of those who have actually touched the manuscript in the course of my work. In particular I would like to thank Raymond Watkinson, who has always so kindly allowed me to plunder the rich store of his knowledge and love of nineteenth-century books and bookmen; I have long been indebted to him for hours of what the uninitiated might take for delightful conversation, but which has unfortunately been unashamed brain-picking on my part. I am hopelessly indebted to Mrs Barbara Edwards, who not only gave me permission to reproduce the pictures she holds in copyright, and permitted me to take my camera's fill of her father's work, but also entertained and instructed me with information regarding her father; she had also the kindness to read my finished manuscript, and to lend me important books. I could scarcely construct an acknowledgement list without reference to my wife, for as the years have passed she has proved to be a real friend, both in regard to the problems of ordinary living and in regard to the problems of work. I would like to thank Patrick Maher for suggestions concerning the bibliography, and John Lewis for reading and commenting on my manuscript. My thanks are due to Doreen Samuel who helped me with the typing, and to Yocki Rhodes-de Lange who assisted me with the humdrum business of checking the manuscript for errors. In personal indulgence, I would like to cast my mind back some years to a golden summer in Brighton, when Sandy Henderson and I spent so many hours copying Rackham's drawings and paintings, partly for gain, partly for love, and partly to arrive at an understanding of the genius of the man.

To those thanks already issued to the staff of libraries mentioned in the Note to the Bibliography, I would like to add further thanks to the staff of the British Library, both in Bloomsbury and Colindale; to the staff at Brighton Public Library, St Bride's Library, and the Library of the Victoria and Albert Museum.

Then, of course, I must acknowledge my vast debt to Arthur Rackham himself, and the expression of this debt must take the form of an apology, for the very nature of my work has compelled me to adopt the role of critic, whilst I am quite sensible that criticism has no real place in art. It is difficult to write a biography of a person, no matter how highly one might admire that person, without occasionally falling into the role of critic. Yet, as Rudolf Steiner so rightly said, 'To be a critic, you must always hate a little. . . . It is uninteresting to show recognition of other people's work—it only becomes interesting when you can be witty at their expense.' I hope that if I have been witty at all, it is not

6

# ACKNOWLEDGEMENTS

at the expense of Rackham himself, for whom my admiration stands very high.

Like all artists, Rackham was disturbed by vociferous criticism of his work, for hatred is disturbing no matter where it is directed, but apart from the minor rebellion which opposed the series of drawings he produced for *Alice*, his work was generally received with obvious pleasure by the majority of people. He was frequently liked, but also frequently misunderstood. Fortunately Rackham's Virgoan nature stood him in good stead, and he was his own most sensible critic. Writing about the influence and role of criticism in the *Bookman*, October 1926, he professed that he had ceased to be really interested in other people's view of his work, and saw little value in criticism. He rounded off this healthy view with a statement which could be taken to the heart of all artists: 'So, when we have put forth our efforts, let us quietly retire to our workshop again and try to do better next time.' With such an attitude of mind before them, all that critics and biographers may hope to do is to slink off into the distance without being seen, leaving the real Rackham where he has always been—dignified and secure in the mastery of his chosen craft.

# MAINLY BIOGRAPHICAL

'THE year 1867 bids fair to keep its promise to the end,' runs a leader for *The Times* in London in the September of that year. Although the leader-writer does not know it, the promise of the year will produce some extremes which may amuse a cynical historian in the future. The artist Sir Edwin Landseer, his mind failing, has just seen unveiled those proud couchant symbols of capitalist expansionism, the four bronze lions in Trafalgar Square, while in the same year, in another public monument of London, not far away, Marx has just received the first published volume of a weighty text about capital. The year has enhanced the life-giving forces of the future as well as it has sapped them: it sees Joseph Lister first announce to the world the principles of antisepsis, which will surely save lives; and it sees Alfred Bernard Nobel take out a patent for his 'blasting gelatin', now better known as dynamite.

'The year 1867 bids fair to keep its promise to the end. It has been the year of the Exhibition, and the triumph of the arts of Peace was not to be disturbed by warlike alarms. There has been no lack of efforts to trouble the serenity of the halcyon weather. There has been scarcely a day in which men's minds were not disquieted by gloomy prognostics.' So proceeds the leader column of *The Times* for Thursday, 19 September 1867, and yet it is a sign of the peaceful tenor of that nineteenth-century life that the same leader would later describe as 'unprecedented in this country within recent times', the rescue on the same day of two Fenian leaders from the clutches of the police by a band of fifty armed Irishmen, at the expense of one dead bystander, two horses, and three wounded policemen. A steamboat collision on the Thames takes up as much interest and space.

The news shows the perennial story of conflicts, contrasts and injustice. At Clerkenwell, one Henry Kemp, a young apprentice, is imprisoned for six weeks in the House of Correction with hard labour, for assaulting his master in a dispute about a rivet. On the same day London is agog because a Member of Parliament, John Hardy by name, is being arraigned for assaulting a man with his gun—on the following day the MP is fined £5 with costs. In the personal columns of the newspapers, 'capitalists' openly advertise themselves with precisely this word which is almost a stigma now. In the personal columns a professional gentleman is offering 20 per cent interest on a £40 loan for six months, whilst just above his entry we find a company prepared to lend sums of between £20,000 and £25,000 for suitable investment. All this at a time when a large office in the East End of London may be rented for £30 a year, and a villa may be had in Brighton for about the same sum. In Switzerland there is a house agent's dream, a castle over a thousand years old, with walls fourteen feet thick, for sale at a snip of £12,500. It is still possible to educate a child, with full board and no extras, for £20 a year. The beautifully lithographed *British Butterflies* of Noel Humphreys, now rare and sought after by bibliophiles, is being offered at the reduced price of fifteen shillings. The *Arabian Nights*, illustrated by Houghton, is newly on the market.

It is halcyon weather, and the Derwent swarms with salmon at this time of the year. Zadkiel's almanack for 1868 is already for sale, promising a further year of progress, and this with a portrait of the Imperial Prince thrown in, information about earthquakes and how to prevent them, as well as news about the Hindu gods, those deities of British India.

Above all this warmth, injustice, life and chaos, four great planets are conjuncting in the sign of Virgo, and at 210 South Lambeth Road, Anne Rackham, the wife of Alfred Thomas Rackham, gives birth to a very Virgoan child, her fourth in a line of twelve, whom she calls Arthur.

This Arthur Rackham was born into a Dickensian world. It was a world which showed some outward signs of disquiet and unrest, as social stratas slipped under magmatic tensions, but it was essentially complacent in outlook, fearing little for the future, and seeking an identity through a gradual and reluctant amelioration of social conditions directed towards some gradual and undefined conception of social evolution. When Rackham died, in 1939, that world was gone, and he left behind a Kafkaesque world in which the 'arts of Peace' had long since been disturbed by warlike alarms. In his lifetime Rackham had witnessed the most far-reaching social changes and upheavals ever forced upon a world in the short span of half a century, and yet the curious fact is that the life and work of this man in no way testifies to these vast changes and alarms.

It is perhaps in this fact that we find the secret of Rackham's artistic success and fame—a secret which may be termed escapism by the less sensitive. Certainly Rackham remained throughout his whole life a kind of innocent abroad in a world gone mad. In the same years that a million bayonets lanced the youth of Europe, Rackham concerns himself with gnomes, kindly dwarfs and fairies. During the whole of his life the tenor of his life and work insists—quietly and perhaps a little too firmly—that the world of fantasy and creative imagination is better than the so-called world of reality.

In essence, heart, outlook and style, Rackham remained a Victorian, with the dreams of a Victorian. One might even be tempted to say that in essence, heart and outlook Rackham remained a child, but this would not be true, except in the very special sense that artists must remain children, to bother themselves with such absurdities as the spirit in a world so obviously material

9

and concerned with things other than the spirit. Rackham stayed a Victorian in the sense that he adamantly refused to witness the splinter, fragmentation and decay of the world around him. And yet, a man who could identify the Fall of Man with the invention of the wheel, as did Rackham, would certainly appreciate the downward trend of the billion wheels and cogs which worked so thoroughly over Europe during his lifetime. We may be sure that he observed, and it is certain that like everyone else he felt despair, but he refrained from comment. He remained secure in the rich world of his imagination quite apart from, if not actually isolated from, the dissolution of world order.

It is to this rich soul-life, much closer in childhood than in later days, that we unconsciously look when we delight in his work: we see not what was, but what might have been. To adapt an image from Chesterton, who is in many ways the literary equivalent of Rackham, this artist is the one who looks to the trees, and suspects that they are not swaying in the wind, but are themselves grotesque though kindly monsters, which in their movement bring the wind into being.

When faced with such a rich imagination as Rackham's it is necessary to appreciate the overwhelming discrepancy between the outer fiction and the inner fact. The conflict between what a man does externally, how he relates to the social and moral life of the world through his acts, and the inner soul-life which lends force and quality to this life is always a fascinating one. Most biographers—when they are able to formulate the problem to which this conflict between the outer fiction and the inner fact gives rise—solve the problem either by ignoring it, or by entering into a silent conspiracy with the reader. This conspiracy is based on the idea that an artist, or indeed any subject of biography, is *understood* once the dates which pin down his body or his works of art have been given and ruminated on. This is no way to reach into the world of an artist, for whom the soul-life should be of greater importance than any matter of external events and dates, yet, presumably because the conspiracy has gone on for so long, and because it demands so little effort from the biographer (and even less effort from the reader), few bother to question the merits of this common biographic method, or even to recognize its structure.

With Rackham this conspiracy simply cannot work. There is too great a conflict in his case between the inner and the outer. There is such a vast discrepancy, stretched tightly over nearly seventy years, between Rackham the artist and Rackham the man, that it is just not possible to pin down the one by describing the antics of the other. His first biographer, Derek Hudson*, might describe him as 'a neat, alert person, tidy, energetic, punctual', and these words would be a true description of his outer world, but they might also be applied to a million other people, and still reveal nothing about the imaginative soul which dwelled within.

* This reference, and all references not explained in the text or in footnotes, may be studied in the bibliography.

This conflict might even be seen in the name Rackham itself, if one is prepared to make the imaginative leap. Perhaps too much has been made of the remote possibility that Arthur Rackham had as a forbear the pirate John Rackham—who was hanged in Jamaica in 1720*—and yet, even were it true, the hint of swashbuckling would link with only half of our own Rackham, for the creative half is frequently daring enough, and would perhaps command a brigantine in pursuit of prey. The other half, the one that might keep accounts 'with Victorian precision', is the careful one, and yet this side we may also trace in the name, for when in later years Rackham bought himself a large farmhouse in Houghton, West Sussex, it was by some curious chance near the village of Rackham. The name of the village was derived from the Old English *Hreāc-hām*, which meant 'place of the hay rick'. With this etymology the forbears of Arthur Rackham appear as those who carefully arranged ricks of hay in the countryside, for here there is order, system and a general feeling of social good. When he knew that he did not have very long to live, it was to that rural ancestry that he turned: he said to his nurse that it would be nice if he could die where he was, under the trees at Limpsfield. And so we may find in the name, which is carried at one extreme under the skull and crossbones of John, and at the other extreme under the hayforks of peasants, the curious oil and water of unrestrained imagination and peasant stolidity which gave us some of the finest illustrations of our period.

The contrast between the external man and the inner life which flowered in his work, is immediately apparent: Rackham was the most practical of people, trustful, reliable, down to earth, realistic enough to run his own business in a difficult profession, and to run it well; yet, within the field of water-colour painting, which is by technique and method a conservative field in which few artists run riot, a brother artist could write of him as 'one of the most inexhaustibly imaginative painters of poetic and grotesque fantasies whom our water-colour school has ever produced'. We might expect an 'ordinary' man to produce ordinary, unimaginative pictures, but in fact the soul-life of Rackham proved too strong for the world in which he lived, and it broke out of its restrictive fetters into his art.

Baldry unconsciously touched upon this important difference between 'reality' and 'fantasy' which separates the man from the artist, and he came to the conclusion that Rackham 'could not remain a realist, for realism would destroy all the spirit and meaning of his art. He cannot confine himself to the

---

* Arthur Rackham's father decided in 1902 to write down his personal recollections, and an appendix which he added to this manuscript, concerning the life and death of the pirate John Rackham, shows that he at least was convinced of the possibility of a connection. I am indebted to the kindness of Barbara Edwards for permission to quote material from this hitherto unpublished document.

Alfred Thomas Rackham deserves more treatment than space here allows. He joined the Civil Service at the age of 24, in 1854, working as a clerk in the Registry of the Admiralty Court. In 1896 he was appointed to be the Admiralty Marshal and Serjeant at Mace of the High Court of Justice. As he himself said, the appointment of Marshal was 'unique in England and has remained so without material alteration for between 500 and 600 years'.

facts that are before him because plain actuality would never satisfy him and would never allow him the scope for expression that he so intensely desires.' Rackham the man dwelt in the sensible world and deeply respected the factual—in comparison with his artistic and gifted wife, he was regarded as the down-to-earth partner—but Rackham the artist dwelled in the fantasy world, and respected the imaginative. For him, no matter what may be said about other lovers and madmen, the two remained quite separate—one an escape from the other. Only Rackham could possibly know which was the escape.

The pinning down of a body is far easier than any attempt to pin down the soul. Our pins are facts, which tack the body into some semblance of order, and it is because of this pinning that most potted biographies read a little like epitaphs. The body is held down, but the soul flies clear away. For this reason, we shall be brief.

Rackham was born on 19 September 1867. From 1879 he studied at the City of London School. In 1884 he made a four-month trip to Australia for reasons of health, and later in the same seventeenth year, he enrolled as an evening student at Lambeth School of Art, intending to earn his living during the day. Towards this end he became a clerk in the Westminster Fire Office in 1885, and he remained there for eight years until he considered it possible to become a full-time artist on the staff of the newly started *Westminster Budget*. Whilst employed full time as a clerk and attending evening classes, he began to draw for other newspapers and magazines, slowly establishing a reputation for illustrating adventure stories and as a generally versatile artist. By the end of the century he had established himself as a good, thoroughly reliable and even exciting illustrator, especially of children's stories, but his success after this time, through books rather than through periodicals, belongs to the greater part of this book and need not detain us here. By 1902 he had applied for the Associateship of the Royal Water-Colour Society, and in the following year he married Edyth Starkie, an artist, whom he had met in Hampstead two years previously. In the same year of 1908 both these ventures came to fruition in his election to full membership of the Royal Water-Colour Society, and the birth of his daughter Barbara. In 1909 he became a member of the Art-Workers' Guild, for which he served on committees and as Master, in 1919, for many years. And during these years, spent partly in the East End of London, partly in Hampstead, with frequent trips to an old country farmhouse in Houghton, Sussex, then later to a new country house in Limpsfield, punctuated with trips abroad on holiday, to Denmark and the United States for business and acclamation, Rackham drew and painted and constructed that world through which we peer into a soul-life all too rare.

An examination of the photographs and portraits of Rackham (figure 1), and a study of contemporaneous descriptions of the artist, easily forces the conclusion that he was really one of his own gnomes in disguise. His writer friend R. H. Ward maintained that Rackham reminded him of a gnome, with his 'very wide and elfish grin', and he adds almost as an afterthought, 'there was

1 The artist photographed *c.* 1910.

something earthy and even elemental about him'. His nephew Walter Starkie likens his face to a wrinkled ripe walnut, and admits in one context that Rackham resembled, even at the young age of thirty, one of the goblins from Grimm, or Rumplestiltskin; in another context, of the cat in *Alice in Wonderland*. That he was a gnome in disguise is a belief which Rackham appears to have fostered with his genial good humour, for he picks himself out in precisely such a role in several of his pictures: he is for example the gnome peering around the tulips in Kensington Gardens (figure 38); he is also the ugly Roman wearing a toga and familiar horn-rimmed glasses, assiduously scrubbing the blackamoor white

13

(figure 2); he is almost of necessity the leader of that curious group who were going to, or coming away from, St Ives (figure 3), whilst his face appears in a large number of pen and pencil sketches throughout his lifetime, always genial, walnut-faced, semi-grotesque, just as it appeared in real life.

His behaviour, however, is not that of a frolicsome gnome but a responsible human being and Rackham's character proves something of an embarrassment to the biographer in its very perfection. This does not, of course, imply that his work did not at time exhibit weaknesses and faults, but it seems that his character had neither. He was loved by all, by the creative and the mediocre, both groups which are renowned partisans for their own causes. He was a loyal friend, a fine husband, a good father, and his ability to plan, his methodical attention to detail and practical matters and his punctilious behaviour leave no flaws in his human commerce. For all his incredible imagination he is no neurotic artist isolated in his own fairy-land dream. His external life is at once reliable, conforming and secure. He was, in the words of Hudson, '. . . a quiet man with simple tastes and an abstemious almost austere attitude to life'. (This austerity Hudson traces to his early life, but many people had a much harder beginning than Rackham and remained less austere.) He was a good organizer, extremely

2 'His new master thought his colour was due to his late owner's having nelgected him, and that all he wanted was a good scrubbing', *Aesop's Fables* 1912

3 'As I was going to St Ives', *Mother Goose* 1913

fond of joining and serving groups, in sub-committees—thus, the high office he held as Master of the Art-Workers' Guild and three years as Vice-President of the Royal Water-Colour Society. He numbered among his friends notable and interesting creative writers and artists of the time, rubbing shoulders with them formally, as in the Titmarsh Club, or in the old-world atmosphere of the Arts Club, and corresponding with many of them in his heavy and curiously un-imaginative literary manner throughout his life. Perhaps he had no time for faults, for his life was very filled with work; certainly, he appears to have led the kind of life which did not permit the faults to surface.

He remained very much a man of the world. He was perhaps critical of the world he saw emerging: certainly it is fitting, or at least consistent, that an individual who considered even bicycles an abomination might find little in New York except too much noise and many friends. We might also expect such a man to avoid the more unpleasant aspects of the Great War, that this might

15

not disturb the fairyland dream; and so the Hampstead volunteer experiences the spree of Sunday trench digging in Essex, whilst the younger sons experience other things in trenches further to the south. His descriptions of bomb craters on Parliament Hill—craters which were mere scratches in comparison with what was to come—are mixed with ruminations on the rate at which the English grass will disguise so rapidly the English lawn, or concern about the inevitable loss of earnings which so effects a freelance artist in a time of crisis. His contribution of a 'war drawing' to the *King Albert's Book* of 1914 is in the traditional 'outrage and glory' emblematic style, weak in execution and unfortunate in colour—it is clear that this brave new world is not for him. The First World War left few people untouched, but Rackham was among the few who were able to ignore it and survive because his own roots, like the roots of his anthropoid trees which are so deeply embedded in the soil of his fairylands, were so firmly entrenched in the past.

In much the same way as the war went by without disturbing Rackham so far as externals were concerned, the great floodtide of the twentieth century carried its turgid mass beside him, and from a closer examination of his work, it seems that it flooded by without his finding the time or the interest to look up from his drawing board.

# EARLY ARTISTIC INFLUENCES

OUR knowledge of Rackham's schooldays is derived from a few letters and from information wedged in the columns around his first drawing for *Chums* in 1893, by way of illustration to an amusing juvenile account of the City of London School ('I need not say that it is the best in the kingdom, since everyone knows it is.') The school by that time stood on the Victoria Embankment, near Blackfriars Bridge, but during the greater part of Rackham's four years, it was located in Cheapside. We have a flashback from this article, and may see Rackham climbing the dark and dirty spiral staircase, wriggling through the trap door to the roof of the school, to get 'the good view of London and its smoke', and perhaps to leave his name scratched on a forbidden turret. But it is the drawings which interest us. They are for the first issue of May 1893, and are pedestrian, even crude—though just about on par with the other pictures which adorn *Chums* in those years. It is hard to believe that nearly nine years had passed since Rackham had left the halls and rooms he illustrates, a school in which he had gained high reputation as a sketcher and painter, especially in the delicate matter of cartoons of teachers, and for drawings done in 'unorthodox hours', and from which he had actually carried off the school prize for art. Rackham had left City of London firmly intending to be an artist, yet he was by temperament too careful to throw himself into the freelance maelstrom without some kind of security.

Nine years later, and in 1893 he was still churning out inferior drawings which show no sign of particular talent, let alone that quality which would eventually rank him as one of the foremost illustrators of his time. By any standards, Rackham proved to be a slow developer, and this clearly stemmed from his own cautiousness in choosing to take a steady job, rather than in committing himself to a full-time art school training. This was apparently a matter of economics. Although the Lambeth School of Art was listed as 'aided', the degree of aid can be judged by studying the published statistics. The grant for the year 1884 was £396.2s.0d: fees paid by students totalled £682.19s.6d. Rackham's father was not poor by Victorian standards of poverty, but he did have a large family to support.

Rackham never had the advantage (or, for that matter, the disadvantage) of a full-time art education. On his return from Australia in September 1884 he enrolled at the Lambeth School of Art, then in Miller's Lane, and with just over 650 students the largest art school in the London area. He then, quite characteristically, took a day job as a clerk in the Westminster Fire Office, where he was to remain for seven years.

At Lambeth he was a part-time student, and we may be sure that the slight official art training he received during that period has been over-estimated. It is unlikely that he had much contact with the full-time students, or had much attention from the better-known teachers. It has been suggested by Hudson that he would have learned from his co-students Charles Ricketts, Thomas Sturge Moore and Leonard Raven-Hill, but this is extremely unlikely. Thomas Sturge Moore, a fine illustrator though a better poet, did not transfer from Croydon Art School to Lambeth until 1887, and it is certain that Rackham had little personal dealing with him; any influence which might suggest Moore in the later work of Rackham is probably from communal sources rather than directly from Moore himself. Charles Ricketts, who 'looked . . . more like a dandylion puff than anything else', was the star of Lambeth in those days, a year senior to Rackham and soon to be a teacher at Lambeth though temperamentally not suited for that role since he was 'always producing collisions and soreness', and yet also one who 'always dealt *en grand seigneur*, a natural aristocrat as well as a loyal and devoted artist'.* Any light from this bright star was reflected only much later in Rackham's own work. There is no certain knowing whether Rackham knew these two gentlemen at that time (although Rackham's daughter told me that they were known to her father in later years), or even the less talented Leonard Raven-Hill, who later worked on the same magazines as Rackham. It seems that Rackham was taught by a much more conservative artist, W. H. S. Llewellyn, who was later to become a success in social life, but who in Rackham's first year at Lambeth had only just had his first picture accepted for the Royal Academy exhibition of that year.†

It is also certain that the clerk Rackham had little to do with that amazing coterie shepherded by the recluse McGuire in the now obliterated Vale off King's Road, Chelsea, a coterie connected with Lambeth and which did more to influence the growth of the arts than any other art school. Here Ricketts and Shannon lived at number one, the walls of the house previously decorated by no less a painter than Whistler, with William de Morgan next door but one, and Reginald Savage later wedged between them. William de Morgan often put up Walter Sickert, and the group attracted the visits of Wilde, Shaw, Yeats, Wilston Steer, the Rothensteins, Roger Fry, Max Beerbohm, Charles Condor, Lucien Pissarro and the like, for tea and talk and other things. This climate was too rare and exuberant for Rackham, and we find no mention of his name in their accounts of this period.

* The first quote from the pen of Sturge Moore himself, the second from that of Bernard Shaw, both taken gratefully from *Self Portrait. Letters and Journals of Charles Ricketts,* edited by Cecil Lewis, 1939.
† Later Sir William Henry Samuel Llewellyn (1858–1941). RA in 1920; PRA in 1928 for ten years; KCVO in 1918 and GCVO in 1931.

4 'A Fact', *Scraps* 4 October 1884

Even eight years later, in 1892 when Ricketts and Moore were well established, Rackham was still plodding on as a full-time clerk in the daytime, and in the evening doing what he called 'much distasteful back work' as a mediocre freelance of the journalistic kind. He had not yet found even that quality of line which was to make him famous towards the end of the century. Certainly, it was not from those people around him during his sporadic art-school period that he learned about drawing, but from the later study of illustrations and reproductions by the master, and from that most excellent of art teachers, the need for unremitting practice and execution in the face of deadlines, even with the awareness of what a casual observer of the time may well have regarded as only ordinary talent.

Much of the work which Rackham produced for such weeklies as *Scraps*, *The Pall Mall Budget* and *The Westminster Budget* show little talent beyond what might be expected of a graphic journalist.* There is, however, a remarkable versatility of vision and execution, ranging from the soft half-tones intended to catch the quality of photographs, to the lively 'Phil May' exuberance of on-the-spot sketches of personalities or incidents in London life from decorative portraits to virtual cartoons. The samples selected at figures 6 to 20 are intended not to demonstrate ability, so much as the versatility of Rackham at that time. All this journalism demanded the training of a rapid eye for detail, a feeling for variety, and a facility of line which would stand Rackham in good stead in later time.

Since so little research has been done into Rackham's early illustrations for newspapers and magazines, it will not be out of place to glance at a few of these

* The earliest Rackhams that I have been able to trace in these weeklies are: *Scraps* 3 October 1884; *Pall Mall Budget* 15 January 1891; *The Westminster Budget* 2 February 1893.

# MUNCHAUSEN CLUB.

By the Editor of *Funny Folks*.

## CHAPTER XLII.

### "LODGINGS FOR TRAVELLERS."

ND the doctor, sure enough, it was. Nobody who had once seen his somewhat duck-like—for he had, to tell the truth, a most decided waddle—his habit of sticking his thumbs in the armholes of his waistcoat, and the peculiar elevation of his double chin in the air, could mistake him. Both Harry and Grumps would have known him a mile off.

He was coming along at a smart trot, and in two or three minutes would be at the lodge gates.

5 Chapter heading for 'The Munchausen Club', *Scraps* 10 January 1885

here. On the whole, the greater number of these early drawings do more to gratify nostalgia rather than to give aesthetic thrills, though a small handful of them do manifest a distinctive quality of their own.

Rackham's earliest published illustration, which appeared in *Scraps* on the 4 October 1884 (figure 4) is crude, even for an eighteen-year-old artist, and shows an equally crude device used by mothers in Ceylon to prevent their children eating too much. In the face of this clumsy handling, it may be surprising to find in an edition of *Scraps* a few months later Rackham's monogram attached to an interesting heading for 'The Munchausen Club', the column which passed for editorial comment (figure 5). This vignette has a delightful innocence and life about it, and the drawing, for all its wood-engraving style, reminds us more of Dicky Doyle than of any Arthur Rackham we shall learn to know in the future.

The work which Rackham did later for *The Westminster Budget* and *The Pall Mall Budget* is uneven, but in some few cases the drawings are really delightful. Generally speaking, the line drawings are on the whole more felicitous than the tone and line and wash pictures (figure 6), mainly because reproductive techniques still could not do full justice to such delicate artwork, and also because tone was not Rackham's true form of expression. Much of his work for these papers was done by way of reportage: at that time all dailies and weeklies had their small bevy of artists as an equivalent of the teams of journalistic photographers of the modern newspapers. Such artists were required to travel to various places—scenes of crime, police courts, fires, and so on—and prepare drawings as documentation or to add visual life to the columns of type. In this capacity Rackham was to find himself one day committed to recording a recent bank robbery (figure 7), which is reduced to an image of a policeman standing outside

6 'Hoity Toity', *Westminster Budget*
9 February 1893

the robbed bank's entrance, and the top-hatted thief accosting the messenger in the lobby of the bank. The next week he found himself in the Royal Palace, charged with drawing the new Prince Edward (17 August 1894) for *The Westminster Budget*. With such varied work as this, which must have contrasted strongly with his experience as a clerk, we may well understand why Rackham at this time looked with such gloom upon his future, for it was obvious to all those involved in journalism that before long the processes for enabling printers to reproduce from photographs would be perfected. With hindsight we see that this threat was to our gain, for there is no doubt that if Rackham had not been forced by exigencies out of graphic reportage, then he may never have gone into book illustration.

7 'How a Bank was Robbed', *Westminster Budget* 9 February 1893

# ARTHUR RACKHAM

The years of reportage left several interesting drawings, though no real sign of genius. It would be possible to produce a monograph of nineteenth century London life from the many drawings which Rackham left at this time, but few of the drawings would merit real attention: those reproduced here between them represent the highest level which his art reached in these years. In *The Pall Mall* for 19 March 1891, we see prefigured the present agony of travel in London—though Rackham's scenes of Oxford Circus suggest a struggle a little more dignified than that which takes place in the Underground morning

8 'The Struggle for Seats—Scenes at Oxford Circus', *Pall Mall Budget* 19 March 1891

9 'The Dog's Swimming Bath on the Embankment', *Pall Mall Budget*
10 September 1891

and evening today (figure 8). In September of the same year he presents a
view of pedestrians being either delighted or disturbed by exuberant wet dogs,
who have just had their bath in the Thames (figure 9): in the next month the
exigencies of journalism carry him through the social hierarchies, and he
provides a drawing, almost in pastiche of Hassell, though before Hassell's time,
of a deified Queen Victoria, and the heavy caption 'with respectful homage to a

10 Silhouettes from the design drawn by Rackham for *The
Titmarsh Club* Dinner of 1909, printed 1925

11 'With our respectful homage to a Lady who doesn't live in a shoe',
'News of the Week', *Pall Mall Budget* 8 October 1891

Lady who DOESN'T live in a shoe' (figure 11). In February of the next year the
streets of London are covered in snow and sleet and slush, and Rackham
provides drawings showing the consequences of such abominable streets—a cab
horse has slipped, and is perhaps downed for ever (figure 12). And so it goes on,
the daily slog of producing drawings, many of which would finally be rejected
for want of space, and those used scarcely seen in their day, and now merely
views into a quaint and long-lost past.

*The Westminster Budget* tends to be a little more literary than the *Pall Mall*,

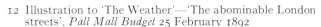

12 Illustration to 'The Weather'—'The abominable London
streets', *Pall Mall Budget* 25 February 1892

13 'The Chicago Ballet at the Alhambra', *Westminster Budget* 14 April 1893

and, what is more important, the art editor appears to have been prepared to give his artists a freer hand with their style. Rackham was frequently still required to provide straight line drawings, but at times he was permitted to inject into his work a little of the so-called 'new style' which was sweeping through the land. The same journal carries a review drawing of the Chicago Ballet Company, which visited England in 1893, and danced at the Alhambra (figure 13), alongside such drawings as 'After a runaway horse' (figure 14) as illustration to 'A Chat with Police-Sergeant X', or the heading for 'The Impres-

14 'After a Runaway Horse', *Westminster Budget* 10 March 1893

15 'A Study in Temptation', *Westminster Budget*
13 July 1894

sionist Protomartyr', both of which indicate in no uncertain way Rackham's penchant for the curvilinear line which was forcing its way back into art. By April 1893 there are such excellent full-page illustrations as that provided by Rackham for Richard le Gallienne's poem 'To Spring' (figure 16), though it is interesting to note that for all its freshness, the time is not yet right for Rackhamerie to emerge, for the trees are not yet humanified, and the hair tresses of the woman are not yet disposed in the fashion characteristic of the Rackham everyone knows. However, in its very unlyrical setting, the drawing does reveal

# To Spring

Is it the Spring?
  Or are the birds all wrong
That play on flute and viol,
  A thousand strong,
In minstrel galleries
  Of the long deep wood,
Epiphanies
  Of bloom and bud.

Grave minstrels those,
  Of deep responsive chant,
But see how yonder goes,
  Dew-drunk, with giddy slant,
Yon Shelley-lark,
  And hark!
Him on the giddy brink
  Of pearly heaven
His fairy anvil clink,

Or watch, in fancy,
  How the brimming note
Falls, like a string of pearls,
  From out his heavenly throat;
Or like a fountain
  In Hesperides,
Raining its silver rain
  In gleam and chime
On backs of ivory girls—
  Twice happy Thyme!
Ah, none of these
  May make it plain,
No image we may seek
  Shall match the magic of his gurgling
    beak.

And many a silly thing
  That hops and cheeps,
And perks his tiny tail,
  And sidelong peeps,
And flitters little wing,
  Seems in his consequential way
To tell of Spring.

The river warbles soft and runs
  With fuller curve and sleeker line,
Though on the winter-blackened hedge
  Twigs of unbudding iron shine,
And trampled still the river-sedge.

And O the sun!
  I have no friend so generous as this sun
That comes to meet me with his big warm
    hands.
  And O the sky!
There is no maid, how true,
  Is half so chaste
As the pure kiss of greening willow wands
  Against th' intense pale blue
Of this sweet boundless, over-reaching waste.

And see !—dear Heaven, but it is Spring !—
  See yonder, yonder, by the river there,
Long glittering pearly fingers flash
  Upon the warm bright air:
Why, 'tis the heavenly palm,
  The Christmas tree,
Whose budding is a psalm
  Of natural piety;
Soft silver notches up the smooth green stem.
  Ah, Spring must follow them,
It is the Spring!

O Spirit of Spring,
  Whose strange instinctive art
Makes the bird sing,
  And brings the bud again;
O in my heart
  Take up thy heavenly reign,
And from its deeps
  Draw out the hidden flower,
And where it sleeps,
  Throughout the winter long,
O sweet mysterious power,
  Awake the slothful song!

RICHARD LE GALLIENNE.

16 'To Spring', *Westminster Budget* 7 April 1893

17 'A Little Holiday in Belgium', *Pall Mall Budget* 16 July 1891

a lyrical side to Rackham's style. This has not yet emerged, of course—presumably because the factual linear approach demanded of his reportage was rarely allowed to enter into his drawings before he took to book illustration. Such drawings show that fantasy was striving to get out even at this stage, but the very rigour of his work required that he should repress it. Perhaps this bottling and pickling of fantasy was the very preparation for those years of maturity, when circumstances permitted Rackham to dispense with reporting the outer reality, and concern himself more with the gentle elaboration of the more convincing inner reality.

It became clear, however, from the profusion of commissions he began to receive from 1892 onwards, that his days as an insurance clerk were numbered. In the following year he felt confident enough to launch himself into the perilous art world, and he joined the staff of the newly launched *Westminster Budget* as a journalistic illustrator. In this post he gained some reputation for his line drawings, especially those of famous personalities of the time, which appeared as features and news items in the magazine. Few of the illustrations of this time need detain us here, for none of them show signs of real promise, or even of good craftsmanship and ability. The first exciting drawings which came of this liaison with *The Westminster Budget* was not for the weekly but for a book: the cover design for *The New Fiction* of 1895, which was a surprisingly good example of his style at that period. The semi *art nouveau* hair style, and the Fuseli-like high drama of the woman, obviously driven to despair by this new fiction, set Rackham at his best at this time. The bold line and strong visual imagery was required as

28

the house style of the Westminster Gazette Library, of which this was a volume, and it shows another direction in which this versatile artist might have gone, had he not been allured by circumstance and inclination into more ethereal fields.

The ethereal fields were slow in emerging, however. Rackham was something of a late developer both as an artist and as an illustrator of books. It is easy, perhaps, to lay the blame for this on his own cautious nature, on the fact that he received no adequate training, or even on the demands made on his time and energy by the graphic journalism of the time. In fact, there is another reason for this late emergence, connected with certain technical developments of the time, and the delaying effect of this we shall examine at a later point (see pp. 36ff. below). Whatever the reasons, however, Rackham was twenty-seven years old when his first book illustrations for the travelogue on the United States by Thomas Rhodes, *To the Other Side*, were published, and it was not until 1896 that his own personal style began to develop and signs of real talent became evident.

It is perhaps a result of a feeling of uneasiness over Rackham's late development and the contrast this makes with his sudden leap into fame, that has led some bibliographers to find evidence of earlier books than the 1893 travelogue of Thomas Rhodes. It has been suggested that Rackham illustrated two books when he was nineteen years old. These are Harriet Beecher Stowe's *A Dog's Mission*, published in 1887,* and *The Ferryman's Boy* by Crona Temple (actually, by Clara Corfield), which appeared in the same year, both under the imprint of Thomas Nelson and Sons.

* This is the date on the titlepage, but the British Library copy is marked November 1886.

18 'The Season of the Growler', illustration
to 'Some Chats with Cabbies', *Pall Mall Budget*
6 August 1891

The ascription to Rackham appears to have been made solely on the basis of a monogram which appears on the eight illustrations for *A Dog's Mission*, and on five of the seven drawings for the second book. Whilst it might be admitted that the monogram (figure 19) in some ways resembles the AR of Rackham's authentic diagram, it will be observed that it may also be read as a compound of AJR, rather than as a simple monogram for AR. A full discussion of the pros and cons of this ascription may not be of great interest to the general reader, and so I have added a few notes in Appendix C, on page 188; for the moment it is worth observing that the thirteen drawings to which this 1887 monogram is affixed are in no way related to Rackham's style of vision as attested at that time in his sketchbooks and surviving drawings. They are clumsy, ill-conceived and unimaginative, and whilst it is quite possible that they may be the work of a young artist, they are certainly the work of a bad and untalented artist, certainly not that of a young man who is to have a water-colour accepted for exhibition at the Royal Academy in the following year. When questioned about his early work by his bibliographer Coykendall, Rackham indicated that *To the Other Side* was his first book, and, whilst we may sympathize with any wish of Rackham to forget such early efforts, we must also recall that he was an exceedingly honest man. The ascription of these books to Rackham cannot stand: the evidence is too flimsy, and the slur on his talent unjustified.

The flowering was sudden, and without familiarity with his many various and versatile styles of magazine drawing during the preceding years, it might

19 Frontispiece to 'A Dog's Mission' by Beecher Stowe. This illustration is almost certainly not by Rackham

20 'The Shirehall and High Street, Chelmsford',
*Sunrise-Land* 1894

be hard to explain the quality of the early books which appeared after 1896, his thirtieth year. The first of these, and by no means the best, was *The Dolly Dialogues* of 1894, which besides a cover gives four rather unpleasant illustrations in his line and wash style. In the same year, however, appeared *Sunrise Land* by Annie Berlyn, to which Rackham provided seventy-three illustrations, all of the vignette type, most of them based on photographs, but in a quality of line which is refreshing in appearance, if a little slovenly in the use of tone, shading and certain architectural details (figure 20). He was not alone in the illustration of this book however, for another artist by the name of Blake had also contributed a large number of drawings, cruder in line than those of Rackham, but sufficiently on par not to disturb the unity of this interesting book.

Rackham's real development cannot be attributed purely to his art-school training, nor solely to natural talent, and yet development took place, for by the end of the century he was established as an artist of real promise, noted especially for imaginative and fantastical line drawings. The list of book reprints (see Appendix B, page 183) of magazine illustrations indicates the degree to which his illustrations were regarded as financially satisfactory from the publisher's point of view. And yet, according to his own account, it was at this time in his career that he experienced the worst tribulations of his freelance artistic life, for as he puts it,

work was hard to get and not well paid, and such efforts as I made along the lines I have since followed received little encouragement. And then came the Boer War. That really was a very thin time indeed for me, and may be considered the worst time I ever had. The kind of work that was in demand to the exclusion of almost all else was such as I had no liking for and very little aptitude. It was also clear that the camera was going to supplant the artist in illustrated journalism, and my prospects were not encouraging.

31

21 Heading vignette from *Cassell's Magazine* 1902

But my work was becoming less immature, and before long my special bent began to be recognized—by artists first. I was elected to membership of one or two exhibiting societies, my work was welcomed, dealers and publishers became interested, and the worst was passed.'*

It comes as something of a shock to realize that this man, who was only a few years later to be eulogized as 'a painter of Fantasies' ('We have no one who can quite be compared with him, no one who uses his particular executive method with a tithe of his ability or approaches him in fanciful originality')† was, just before the turn of the century, still feeling insecure in his chosen career as nothing better than a journalistic hack. In retrospect it all looks very different now, for within a decade he was the most famous and sought-after illustrator of fantasy books, with an exquisite control over line and design.

The changes which came over his ability and art in that decade may be understood only by examining the real sources of his art education, imaginative grasp, and improvement of linear control—the other books and magazine illustrations which were being produced by his most talented contemporaries. Rackham learned more from these other pictures than from any living person, or from any number of evening hours in Lambeth School of Art. Sturge Moore, in describing the art-school scene in later years, supports this argument when he mentions the collections of illustrations made by his own group—the illustrations by the 'Pre-Raphaelites, Boyd Houghton, Keene, alongside of Villette and Menzel or Blum, Brennan, Howard Pyle and Abbey . . .' Later he added the throwaway but important line, 'But there were others merely collected as cribs.'‡ Anyone interested in tracing the major sources of such influences and cribs on Rackham might like to study the work of Howard Pyle, Archie MacGregor, Alice B. Woodward and especially the work of J. F. Sullivan and Charles Robinson. Specific titles which show traits followed by Rackham may be given as follows: Howard Pyle, *The Wonder Clock*; MacGregor, *Katawampus*; Alice B. Woodward, *Red Apple and Silver Bells*; Woodroffe, *Nursery Rhymes*; Sullivan, *The Flame Thrower*; and Charles Robinson, *King Longbeard*. Probably Rackham also looked closely at the numerous wood engravings drawn by Maclise for Moore's *Irish Melodies*, for in these the gothic impulse,

*The Bookman October 1925. 'The Worst Time in my Life', a short article by Rackham.
†A. L. Baldry 'Arthur Rackham: A Painter of Fantasies *The Studio* May 1905.
‡Gwynn *Sturge Moore and the Life of Art,* London 1952.

22 'Hey! up the chimney, lass! Hey after you!', *The Ingoldsby Legends* 1907

which interweaves animals, humans, plants and stones with complex traceries of plant and scrollwork borders, must have sparked off Rackham's imagination frequently. In fact, those who would largely trace Rackham to Dickie Doyle might well step back in surprise when they examine a few of these sources.

# ARTHUR RACKHAM

If we catch a glimpse of Boyd Houghton's Arabian women in Swift's land of giants, if we see a little Cruikshank in the swirl of a witch's broomstick (figure 22), or find the embryonic forms of Rackham's tree-gnomes in Maclise, we may be tempted to believe that we have caught Rackham's 'source'. But in this belief we would be wrong. Rackham had no single graphic or painterly influence on his work or life; he grew from that richest of all traditions, which is so frequently sneered at by the ignorant: the journalistic graphic tradition.

The chief advantage of the little-understood and the maligned journalistic influence is that it does not over-rate originality, as does the 'fine art' world, with the result that the technical competence of the artist is allowed to flow and grow at the right natural pace. Thus, few graphic artists say anything of importance in their work until they are old enough and mature enough to have something worth saying. Besides this remarkable advantage, there is the added fact that the energy source for the journalistic graphic tradition is to be found not in one or two single focal points, but in the leaf-drift of centuries, since all great works of art are eventually popularized and then assimilated into the soil of our culture by means of the impulse which started in Europe with Gutenberg. Rackham was heir to this tradition, rather than a debtor to one person or to a small group, and it is to that tradition that we would have to look were we to understand fully the early influence which flowered so beautifully during the next century.

# TECHNIQUE AND STYLE

RACKHAM slowly developed into what a modern advertising agency would call 'a good line man'. His best and worst plates are quite definitely 'coloured drawings' rather than painterly illustrations, and their emphasis is generally on quality of line. Of course, Rackham's best plates so combine drawing with colour that an exquisite pitch is reached in which one cannot be separated from the other without detriment to both, but with the colour he is, as Julian Garner puts it, frequently 'more interested in tone relationship than variety of hue'.* In many cases it is possible imaginatively to strip out the colour in one deft sweep, and find a highly satisfactory line drawing which the colour and tone had tended to hide.

That Rackham should be a good line man is scarcely surprising in view of the many years he spent in enforced apprenticeships with newspapers and comics, and then in more willing service with periodicals such as *Little Folks*, preparing line drawings and the occasional 'photographic wash', always with obvious enthusiasm for the line and clear distaste for the wash. Rackham was already established as an artist of considerable ability before any of his illustrations were reproduced in colour. Indeed, the first colour picture to appear was significantly enough a coloured version of a line drawing which he had done in 1896, his thirtieth year, the frontispiece for the delicious *Two Old Ladies, Two Foolish Fairies and a Tom Cat* (figure 23), which appeared in 1897. His fame as a colourist did not come until 1905, with *Rip Van Winkle*, but for a decade before that he was highly regarded as a serious line illustrator.

Rackham clearly thought first of all in line, and only secondly in colour, so that the majority of his plates may indeed be described (and not unkindly) as 'coloured line drawings'. Those who bracket the work of Rackham with that of Edmund Dulac, who is essentially a colourist, fail to understand the real nature of Rackham's personal vision and technique.

Rackham's background, training and temperament—even his actual technique used in producing the coloured plates—drove him to conceive the world around him in terms of line, and of illustrations as coloured line drawings. This

* Julian Garner 'The Wizardry of Arthur Rackham' *International Studio* July 1923.

35

linearist attitude, which perhaps explains his penchant for trees, roots, wrinkled faces and all such things which may be represented in fluid line, is peculiarly revealed in his giving permission for another artist to colour some of his early line drawings for use in a book. Rackham gave permission for the illustrator Harry Rowntree to colour six of the pictures in Maggie Browne's reprint of the stories originally from *Little Folks* (1901), in *The Book of Betty Barber*. There are signs, though no literary showing, that the coloured plates going under Rackham's name in several other titles were by 'other hands', and these of little expertise. A reissue of Harriet Martineau's *Feats on the Fjord* in 1914 contained eight of Rackham's original line drawings which had been coloured by Cubitt Cooke. For several years after he had established himself as an artist with international appeal and repute, he continued to issue coloured versions of early drawings, with the line of these scarcely changed, save where the exigencies of such printing or reproduction required such change. It is clear from such examples that he felt confident with his line, and regarded colour as something 'additional', something which might improve, but which would never in itself complement a weak drawing.

One important reason why Rackham was able to exploit his personal line during the last decade of the nineteenth century is bound up with certain developments in mechanical means of reproduction which had developed in

23  Frontispiece, 'Dancing Round and Round', *Two Old Ladies, Two Foolish Fairies and a Tom Cat* 1897

24 Preliminary pencil drawing for an
illustration to *Don Quixote*, which Rackham
wanted to illustrate but for which
he never received a commission.

that period during which Rackham was beginning to find his feet as an artist. In a previous decade an illustrator would have been required to submit his line drawings to a wood-engraver, who might well have pasted down the original pictures on to his boxwood block, and then cut into it with his burin. Under such circumstances the artist, a proud beast at the best of times, found himself at the mercy of craftsmen engravers, and tempers frequently ran high. One of the most accomplished of English painters of Victorian England told Henry Blackburn in the early nineties that when he first drew for illustration, the wood-engraver dictated the angle and style of cross-hatching, so as to fit the engraver's tools.* The engraver freely interpreted the drawings given to him, and the best Victorian wood-engravings are always a result of a felicitous relationship between artists and engravers.

There are fewer things which give such a sense of exhilaration to the historian of graphics than the liberation of individual linear style which occurs during the last decade of the nineteenth century, due exclusively to the improvements of mechanical reproduction which ousted the engraver as an interpreter. The improvements began with what was then called the 'photo-zinc process', which involved the use of photography of line drawings, these being transferred to a zinc-faced block, later to be etched mechanically with acids. The method, whilst it had certain draw-backs, interfered little with the quality of the artist's line in the necessary production of a relief block for printing purposes. One of the earliest instructional manuals on the methods of drawing for mechanical

* Henry Blackburn *The Art of Illustration*, 1893.

LIFEBOAT HOUSE, WELLS.

and was launched on
July 10th, 1882, by
Miss Charlotte Nichols.
This was superseded in
July, 1888, by another,
named the "Baltic,"
fitted with all the latest

25 'Lifeboat House Wells', *Jarrold's
Guide to Wells-next-the-sea* 1894

reproduction, a book which Rackham must surely have read, is *The Art of
Illustration* by Henry Blackburn, which sounds the knell of commercial wood-
engraving, and heralds the new age of individualized line: 'As there is no
question that the handwork of the artist can be seen more clearly through
mechanical engraving than through wood engraving, it behoves him to do his
best.' It was into such a climate that Rackham, at heart a linearist in any case,
was maturing. A study of his early newsprint drawings show that the very
earliest were produced under the hand of the engraver, yet within the year his
work was being produced through photo-mechanical means, and he was thus
free to produce line drawings which would be faithfully reproduced down
to the smallest dot or linear flexion. It was in fact a mechanical invention more
than any other single factor which permitted the flowering of so many highly
individual English illustrators at the end of the nineteenth century.

By the first colour work of 1896, Rackham had developed the control over
line to such an extent that he was permitted a versatile expression in a wide
variety of fields. His line was capable of being informative and descriptive,
without at the same time being 'mechanical' or boring, as in the topographical
drawings he produced from photographs for Annie Berlyn's *Sunrise Land* in
1894. The line might be delicate and fluid, as in the many fairy pictures he
produced for *Little Folks* (figure 86), or at the other extreme, robust and richly
textured, as in the images of energetic gnomes and dragons (figure 44). Again
for all the fluidity of handling that was within his grasp, he was also capable of
the more careful handling of pen required of the rhythmic and decorative
drawings which he made within the style so erroneously called *art nouveau*
(figure 16). By this time the ultimate line drawing, the silhouette, had been
explored, though it was still to be developed and refined to the exquisite standard
he achieved in a later period.

# TECHNIQUE AND STYLE

A survey of the period's magazines and books, or even of the few listed on pp. 20–28 above, will indicate that other artists also used line as well, and we must therefore be prepared to indicate what is special about the line of Rackham, if we are to understand more fully his style and method of working. With Rackham the line is itself almost a delicate root tendril spreading over the paper, its growth creating an organic form which is so distinctive in quality, feeling and even subject matter that a special word is required to hint at its peculiarity. A portmanteau word runs easily off the tongue, and *Rackhamerie* serves the purpose well, for as a word it rolls into one the hints of hampsters, or other species of gentle, humanoid mice-like creatures, and a genial camaraderie which exudes confidence. The neologism is intended to encompass gnarled anthropomorphized trees and gib-nosed gnomes wriggling within the roots of these same trees, upon the branches of which perch birds of a plumage and form not to be found in the present world of reality. Rackhamerie also connotes fairies, though not insipid fairies (because other artists have drawn such kinds), as well as gnomes and mice and humanoid birds: in fact, Rackhamerie must be taken as a more specific term for what has been called neo-gothic, that specially muted, other-world vision, in which the tangle of tree-roots, scroll interweavings of tendrils, shoots and ferns, merge with the legs, arms, bodies and absurd clothes of a hundred grotesque gnomes, who so combine to flood the roots with animal magnetism that the trees themselves are galvanized into life. And all these transformations and transmutations are worked through by the magic of line, so that line and image become inseparable within the organic unity of the whole.

26 'They met many a quaint creature', *The Rainbow Book* 1909

Such a well-filled portmanteau word might easily slide into sentimentality, in a way that a term such as 'Rembrantesque' may be said merely to echo the middle-class sense of security through material possessions, to those who know nothing of art, or in the way 'Kafkaesque' may merely imply intense bureaucratic persecution, to those who know nothing of the human condition. Fortunately, the thing which prevents the neologism from becoming sentimental is the work of Rackham itself, for whilst it is easy for one to indulge in sentimentality whilst *thinking* or *talking* about Rackham's images, it is quite impossible to be sentimental when faced with them.

27 From *The Book of Betty Barber* 1910

The line is organic Rackham, and it is the soul which finds expression through the line which we may call Rackhamerie. Already we have been removed by words from the banal 'advertising agency' description of Rackham as a good line man, and quite properly so, for he is more than merely that. However, a study of the line and the soul-life to which the line gave rise, throws some light on Rackham's method of working, the structure and concepts within many of his pictures.

Rackham would begin his pictures by sketching carefully with a soft pencil the broad outlines of the composition either working on card, or on a good quality, slightly textured, paper mounted on card. From fairly early times, even when illustrating children's stories for magazines, he began to establish a repertoire of compositional devices which served him well in the future, and which lend their own stamp to many of his plates (see pp. 66ff. for a survey of the major compositional devices used by Rackham). He presumably visualized the images he intended to create on paper in terms of one or other of a set and limited number of compositional devices, and blocked in the chosen one into the picture area to act as the salient structure for the important lines. Into this he would work his figures or emotive points of interest. This method of working— from the established mass down to the details within the mass—remained with Rackham throughout his life, and if we examine Rackham's pictures correctly we actually see them in this way, from the mass down to detail. Anyone familiar

28 'The Quack Frog', *Aesop's Fables* 1912

You spotted snakes with double tongue,
  Thorny hedghogs, be not seen;
Newts & blind-worms, do no wrong,
  Come not near our fairy queen.
  Philomel, with melody
    Sing in our sweet lullaby;
Lulla, lulla, lullaby, lulla, lulla, lullaby:
    Never harm,
    Nor spell nor charm,
  Come our lovely lady nigh;
  So, good night, with lullaby.

29 'You spotted snakes with double tongue', *A Midsummer Night's Dream* 1908

with Rackham will continue to discover interesting details within plates, within the general compositional masses, which surprise long after they would have considered themselves 'familiar' with the plate.

He appears to have worked about 'two-up', which is to say that his original pictures were about twice the size intended for reproduction purposes. This, however, was not an invariable rule, and in some cases pictures were enlarged and reduced by publishers without reference to Rackham. As his fame grew, he found that it was possible to sell the originals for considerable sums, with the result that he tended to work a little larger, sometimes reaching 'three-up'.

In some cases, before making compositional drawings he appears to have made one or two preparatory studies and sketches of details within the picture. Rackham's fantasy required a sure foundation in the physical world, around which he might construct the lineaments of his other world. This is why so frequently within his pictures we recognize in different plates the same tree (the living version of which stood in his garden at Houghton), and portraits of his friends, his wife and child, not to mention his own impressive face, for he needed live models even for his grotesqueries. From a series of such studies and sketches, and from memory of such, he worked out the large masses of his composition in pencil. Into the general mass of pencil drawing he would then work with pen and indian ink, and once the basis of his drawing had begun to emerge in ink, he cleaned off the pencil drawing beneath.

If the picture were intended for colour reproduction, he might at this stage give a light wash of colour to the whole of his drawing area, according to some authorities to pull together the colour. According to others, however, the aim of

30 'They will certainly mischief you', *Peter Pan in Kensington Gardens* 1906

31 Original drawing by Rackham used in *Fairy Tales of the Brothers Grimm* 1900

this wash was to add an 'antique' or 'olde worlde' effect to the plate. Actually, an artist who has proceeded to colour with thin washes of water-paint a black ink drawing on white paper will understand and sympathize with Rackham's procedure on technical grounds: the point is that the contrast between black ink and white paper is so strong that it tends to render the first applications of colour wash weak or 'bitty'. A wash of tone over the whole drawing certainly helps to pull together the colour, and although it mutes down the range of tonal and hue contrasts, it adds a delicacy of tone, and helps at the same time to integrate the black line work with the colour, for the intermediate wash belongs exclusively to neither, and yet is related to both. This would seem to be an excellent device for any artist who regards the production of colour illustrations as largely a matter of colouring line drawings. At any event, these technical

32 Preliminary conte drawing (with touches of white impasto water colour)
for an illustration to *Don Quixote*, never published

considerations, so essential for an artist working under pressure of time, as did
Rackham, are probably the reasons why his thin washes of brown, bistre or
sepia give the characteristic vellum-like appearance to some of his plates.

Rackham tended to work sparingly with his application of colour—he
worked mainly in a water-colour technique rather than in gouache, and it was
exceedingly rare for him to create even small impastos in his illustration work.
An exception to this may be the original artwork for the plate 'Up a Tree' which
appeared in *Little Folks* in 1899. This well-printed reproduction, which is the
earliest colour work to be reproduced in colour (rather than being originally a
line drawing in inception) appears to have been painted entirely in gouache, and
with considerable light impasto work. This technique was almost immediately
abandoned for reproductive work, and the majority of his pictures are built

33 'Up a Tree', colour illustration from *Little Folks* July 1899

from delicate washes of colour, which have been run over the top of underlying washes, much in the manner of the glazing technique of the oil painter, though, of course, without anything of the rich effect that the oil technique offers.

For technical reasons it is not possible to work many washes of water-colour over the same area, without losing much of the freshness and spontaneity of handling for which water-colourists are famed, and for which the technique is especially adapted. The gum arabic, or the gum tragacanth, which is the binding agent in water-colour is soluble, and thus dissolves when a further wet application

46

is laid on top of it. This was probably one of the contributing factors which led Rackham to adopt a fairly restricted range of hues on his palette, and persuaded him to work mainly towards achieving a varied but monochromatic effect which was relieved and enlivened by subtle contrasts of translucent blues, oranges and bright hues (figure 125). Even by 1922 it was regarded as an 'old charge' that Rackham's palette was subdued, though it was defended by Martin Birnbaum* on the grounds that the salient characteristic of Rackham's art was its gothic spirit—a fair defence, for the gothic and neo-gothic strive to be mysterious, gloomy and permeated with a surface fantasy.

It is this insistence on the neo-gothic side of Rackhamerie that has led many people to believe that this was his sole method of working. However, the wide range of styles and the versatility of Rackham's colour work shows to what extent he was capable of meeting the exigencies of illustration on many fronts. There was almost a technical reason why he should choose to work within the neo-gothic monochromatic darkness, but even in books where such illustrations predominate, one finds colours of a jewel-like intensity, in pictures which are Rackham to the last short flourish of his signature. The significance of the gothic darkness would be missed if it were not seen in relation to the effect it permits with touches of these colours which enliven the whole, and set delicate moods and nuances to the pictures. Rackham was quite capable of using a bright

*Frederick Coykendall *Arthur Rackham: A List of Books Illustrated by Him* New York 1922. Introduction by Martin Birnbaum.

34 Watercolour sketch. Not used in any reproduced work

35 Water colour from *The Pied Piper* printed in the catalogue for the exhibition on the centenary of Rackham's birth, Columbia University, 1967

or a soft palette, though his natural bent, which shunned things that clash, and tended towards the sombre fusion of muted colours, was often relieved by a love for pastel hues.

Some of Rackham's preparatory water-colour sketches, in which he worked out certain of the problems raised by his illustrative themes and compositions, have a delightful quality of handling, though few of the originals have been reproduced. Most of these are now in private collections scattered throughout the world (but see notes on page 190), and are not available for general public inspection, which is unfortunate for they represent a side of Rackham's talent which is not widely known. Two such representative works were reproduced in the catalogue for the important exhibition arranged by Columbia University to mark the centenary of Rackham's birth, in 1967.* One of these, plate V in the catalogue, plate 35 here, is a subject from *The Pied Piper*, in which the washes and blobs of warm greys metamorphose into rats streaming towards an expressionist, Nolde-like face which is part human, part animal and part ghost— a compelling vision of which Kafka himself would have approved. There is a delicious fluidity of handling, and a magic of macabre vision in this sketch which makes it one of Rackham's best preparatory illustrations.

Rackham's attitude to colour in the 'fine art' sense, in relation to his water-colour painting, as distinct from his illustrative work, was a curious one. Though

* Roland Braugham *The Centenary of Arthur Rackham's Birth* New York, 1967.

36 'And a fairy song', *A Midsummer Night's Dream* 1908

49

37 'Elfin Revellers', Plate 28 of *Arthur Rackham's Book of Pictures* 1913

he gained a fine reputation as a water-colour painter, many of his pictures were in many respects highly derivative, and suggest that outside his own domain of fantasy and illustration he was essentially an eclectic who had not found his own personal vision. Examples of such works as were regarded as 'serious fine art' have not been frequently reproduced, but it is possible to indicate from those pictures which Rackham refers to as 'Langham sketches', this derivative and eclectic tendency. These sketches were done at the Langham Sketching Club, which was organized by the Artist's Society, and met within the chambers of the Society on Friday evenings, 'from the first Friday in October till the second Friday in May'. There were about fifty members in the group, all admitted by ballot. Rackham, always a keen club man, appears to have attended the painting group regularly, and to judge from the eagerness with which he reproduced some of these sketches in his *Book of Pictures*, 1913, we must assume that he was well satisfied with what he produced on these Friday evenings. The last two plates in his book are Langham sketches, and illustrate very well Rackham's tendency to be openly derivative, for *Hauling Timber* is very much in the style of George Clausen, whilst *The Regent's Canal* is in essence a Whistler—a very unlikely combination to find associated with one brush.

Some of Rackham's pastoral water-colours have a lovely delicacy of colour, however, and while he showed considerable ability in the use of crisp-edged floods of wash, this technique was well established in the English water-colour school, and may also be classed as derivative. The oil painting *Self Portrait* which hangs in the Art-Workers' Guild, London, is an amateurish affair, clumsy in composition, awkward in drawing, and were it not for the face portrayed, it would be difficult for anyone to associate this with the brush of the fairyteller. For all his expressed wish to be a good oil painter, it is evident that his real strength in paint lay more with gums than oils.

It might be argued that Rackham's early experiences with the difficulties and shortcomings of the three-colour process led him to restrict his use of colour in illustration work. As the early methods generally involved a considerable loss in hue, the natural tendency of an artist familiar with this was to intensify the colour and hue of his original artwork, in order that the loss would still leave a brighter colour in the printed reproduction. This was precisely the manner in which that pioneer process-colourist Howard Pyle worked, and in which Edmund Dulac painted well into the present century. Rackham appears to have reasoned otherwise, for he worked within both a restricted hue-range and a restricted tonal range, so that there would be little noticeable loss in the final reproduction. When the ink drawing had been coloured in with washes of water paint, Rackham would sometimes strengthen some of his lines by drawing over the picture once more with pen and ink.

In discussing the new three-colour process, Blackburn listed as one of the chief faults of the method the fact that 'crispness of detail is often lost, and so in the original there should be no lack of decision to counteract this tendency.' It is almost as though Rackham took these words to heart, for the very purpose of his second ink drawing on top of his coloured illustrations was to strengthen the whole for block-making. This is one reason why in some of the original paintings, the top flourishes of heavy and shiny dried indian ink are so offensive: they are intended to be too strong so that they will be lost and will integrate within the colours and underlying drawing of the reproduced work. Rackham was ever the craftsman, and worked diligently for reproduction of a fine order: his frequently reported difficulties with block-makers have been over-emphasized, and his aim was the same as theirs—to make good colour reproductions.

We have dwelled at some length on Rackham's obvious penchant for line, and since it is in line that he succeeds as an illustrator, we may be tempted to pass by his early failures, which were not directly concerned with line. The failures arose from the need for Rackham to produce illustrations in a technique which was far from congenial to him. In particular the failures are those involving monochromatic tone work which was totally alien to his linearist nature.

In his early days, Rackham was frequently required to prepare artwork in a technique which one may politely call 'photographic wash', but which Blackburn more bluntly called 'lath and plaster', though not in direct reference to Rackham. In this technique, which was surprisingly popular towards the end of the nine-teenth century, the artist prepared a monochrome painting, usually in a semi-photographic style (sometimes in fact using photographs as a guide, for reference, or for the sake of ease and speed of working), in which forms were picked out in contrasts of tone, rather than in contrasts of line. Such a tonal picture was then handed over to the mechanical engraver for block-making, through a method which is now called half-tone process, but which in Rackham's

51

38 'When he heard Peter's voice he popped in alarm behind a tulip',
*Peter Pan in Kensington Gardens* 1906

39 'Certain biscuit-bakers have gone so far as to imprint his likeness
on their new-year cakes', *Rip van Winkle* 1905

53

40 'The lady with the balloons, who sits just outside', *Peter Pan in Kensington Gardens* 1906

early days was more commonly called the Meisenbach process. In simple terms, the method of making relief blocks which would simulate a variety of tones, rather than print merely a single black-line contrast of black and white, was achieved by the process engraver placing a fine screen between the artwork and the camera at the photographic stage. This broke up the continuous tone into a multitude of small dots, the size of which (and therefore also the printing intensity) was determined by the strength of the tone from which it was derived. The painting image was thus turned into an effectual 'line' image with minute and regular dots in the place of continuous tone. At a distance of the few inches

54

which normally separated the reading eye from the page these minute dots merged and gave the impression of a continuous tone which in some respects 'echoed' the tone of the original artwork.

The method was fairly described by Blackburn as 'most ingenious and valuable . . . but which in common use has cast a gloom over illustrations in books and newspapers'. The method obviously cast a gloom over Rackham too (see figure 83). All the many half-tone drawings of the 'photographic wash' style are much of a muchness and were obviously produced by line-man Rackham with great reluctance. In fact, so banal* is the style of these pictures that it is surprising to find him being commissioned to illustrate books requiring by their own style and appeal such a method of illustration, for there were many artists more capable of coping with the demands of photographic work than was Rackham.

In many of his early illustrations, especially those for *Little Folks* magazine, Rackham used the newly developed method of adding tone through the use of pen. In many cases the mechanical tone technique was resorted to as a time saver, as for example in figure 14 (which is typical of this method), but in other cases the mechanical dot was used in order to impose a second colour on the basic drawing. The main dangers inherent in the method (besides the obvious one of the mechanical quality which the method lent to the reproduction), was that the areas to be shaded were actually prepared by the block-maker from an outline sketch provided by the artist in blue pencil. This meant that the artist would rarely see the effect he was imposing upon his own drawing until that dread moment of printing, or at the proof stage, when limitations of time and money prevented drastic alterations.

Rackham's sense of composition is almost as personal as his use of line, and we must examine certain of his compositional methods in detail to reach a full understanding of his art. It is essential to observe that just as the neo-gothic tendency finds its expression in free curvilinear line, and in almost obsessive detail, so does the neo-gothic prefer the vignette to the compositional frame. Rackham at all times shows a tendency to be the artist of the vignette, rather than the artist of the compositional picture. It is proper to contrast the two, for strictly speaking a vignette is a design or illustration on a paper space, having its edges shaded off into the surrounding paper. The term is frequently misused nowadays, and restricted to a virtual synonym for tail-piece or head-piece. In fact, tail- and head-pieces may be vignettes, but they need not necessarily be. (The term was used as a transitive verb by certain early photographers, to describe the act of shading away a background so as to isolate a picture from a hard-edged frame. There was even such a device as a 'vignetter', a photographic screen with a central hole so arranged as to allow a steady increase in opacity to a totally dark periphery.) Without pushing terminology and definition too far, vignettes are distinguished by not having hard-edge borders.

*Notable exceptions are some of the plates he contributed to the 1895 Washington Irvings (see bibliography page 173).

41 'There was one who seemed to be the commander', from *Rip van Winkle* 1905

42 'The Sea Serpent', Plate 25 of *Arthur Rackham's Book of Pictures* 1913

Here we reach the nexus of an important point in Rackham's style: his nordic, neo-gothic spirit drove him to the free, rough-edged vignette, yet he was required by many factors—technical, aesthetic and commercial—to compose pictures within a frame. Rackham was not merely a gothic artist, he was also an English artist, with the two important qualities which have informed all good English art: *individuality*, and what we may term, *anti-classical* feeling. It is a classical urge to compose pictures and images within a rectangular frame, and it is one which has always been weak in English artists; it was certainly weak in Rackham, as the curvilinear gothic style seeks always to liberate itself from the restriction of frames. This is one reason why many of his early line

43  Illustration from 'Stories from the Edda', *Little Folks* 1901

44 'What a glorious ride that was!', *The Rainbow Book* 1909

drawings for *Little Folks* and other periodicals were so successful, for they were not composed into a border, but were relatively free within the setting of the page. In many cases in which Rackham used his early vignette line drawings in the formal coloured plates demanded by books, the original line suffers, not merely because the colour affects it, but because the vignette looks cramped and confined within the strictures of a border. A fine example of this demotion from line vignette to coloured plate may be seen in the transformation of figure 44 to plate 42.

45 '"Preposterous!" cried Solomon in a rage', *Peter Pan in Kensington Gardens* 1906

46  'They all crowded around it panting, and asking, "But who has won?"'
*Alice's Adventures in Wonderland* 1907

61

Rackham was very much aware of this problem, and he solved it most unusually by simply dropping his vignettes into a frame, in as exciting a manner as possible, but having done so, leaving them there for better or for worse. In some rare cases he went to great lengths (figure 41) to arrange his vignettes within a formal composition, but in general his gothic spirit rebelled at the task, and for this reason many of his linear transformations are compositionally unsound.

With Rackham we are continually reminded that the celtic nature, the gothic fantasy, is too turbulent to be contained. The floriated scrolls of the medievalists are not cramped into frames, and are themselves too full of

47 'The Pussy Cat Caught Hold of Her, The Owl Jumped on Her Shoulder', *The Book of Betty Barber* 1910

exuberance to act merely as borders but create a mood and quality of their own. When the medieval painters and illuminators put knights and horses or sinners and saints in borders, they often managed to break out: a sword shaft sticks out here, a horse leaps through there, and a whole medley of heads peep out at the top. The medieval artist inherited the so-called Ringerrike, Jellings and Urnes styles, and from them created their own distinctive scrollwork, among which foliation we find human beings, animals and birds in a perfect unity of graphic form. It was this feeling for vignette and border, for chaos of life as opposed to the stillness for which rectilinear classicism seeks, which Rackham inherited and took to heart.

48 'I put my hands in my trouser-pockets and strode resolutely forward', *Cassell's Magazine* 1903

The vignette is a nordic device with a respect for the page, which is why the dour north-countryman Thomas Bewick was happier leaving his pictures free of rectangular borders, and at his most uncomfortable when attempting to confine his animals, trees and human forms into a frame. Bewick, like Rackham, was turning to the past in his respect for the page: he was claiming in his work that illustration should not be a hole in the page, but an embellishment of its surface. They were both claiming that the nordic genius does not like the picture frame, but clings to the surface, to decoration and the ragged shades of vignette.*

*The technical innovations of Bewick (1753–1828) in regard to the vignette have rarely been appreciated. His use of the end of the wood, with his white line, (wood-engraving instead of wood-cutting) made it possible for the hard-edge border of wood and metal printing to be dispensed with within certain limits. Lithography was only just developing as Bewick worked his vignettes, and the woodblock of the cutter required a border to support the block under the tremendous pressure of the old printing presses. The wood-engraver permitted a return to the free, luxurious, jagged edge of the vignette on the printed page. Vignette with the copper plate was possible but clumsy.

49 'The Hare and the Tortoise', *Aesop's Fables* 1912

The following poem text appears within the illustration:

WHEN I was five, delirious joy
Roused me at dawn, a panting
To rifle thee for sweet and toy,
My stocking.

I fondly dreamed that Santa Claus,
Agent of supernatural laws,
Of thy profusion was the cause,
My stocking.

Tops, marbles, knives, soft gingerbread,
Tin soldiers, weak about the head,
Filled thee, and overflowed the bed,
My stocking.

No cornucopia of old,
Nor purse of Fortunatus bold,
More wealth than thine did e'er unfold.
My stocking.

Nor unforgotten was the "sell,"
Salt tablet for sweet caramel,
A trap wherein I darkling fell,
My stocking.

Methought the jest became the sprite
Whose charioteering chimney-flight,
Filled thee with gems of pure delight
My stocking.

Then, seizing on the hoard, what bliss
To rush and show, with sticky kiss,
That mother, who took naught amiss,
My stocking.

Arrived at nine, too much I knew,
Apace the tree of knowledge grew,
And, ingrate, I derided you,
My stocking.

50  Illustration 'To my Stocking' from *Cassell's Magazine* 1902

Rackham took well to the interlacing and fantasy of the neo-gothic, which was itself born of line, and almost without exception his best early line drawings avoid the use of frame: they are vignettes, or they are integrated into the text (figures 48 and 50). Rackham's first printed colour picture was the frontispiece for *Two Old Ladies* (figure 23), originally a black and white line drawing of 1886, and although now forced into a frame, containing at least one major participant who wishes to break loose from the confines of the frame with shoe and cape. Rackham was never happy with the confining effects of a picture frame, though he developed several simple compositional devices to aid him in coming to terms with it. The attraction of many of his illustrations for children lies not merely in the competence and charm of the line, or even in the rough textures and bizarre imagery, but in the way in which the drawings fill the space and frequently crop into the type area of the columns. The lovely title for the exuberant movement of 'The Dream Picture' (figure 51) of 1896 is a good example of this, though almost any of the illustrations for *Little Folks* would serve as an example of this truth.

51 Heading for 'The Dream Picture' in
*Cassell's Magazine* 1896

The gems of illustration in the *Zankiwank,* also of 1896, would have suffered appallingly had they been confined within even a single line frame, for half their charm lies in their respect for the white space of the page, and for the rhythms which Rackham established on the open face of white.

Confronted with obvious artistic and temperamental difficulties in regard to composition, it appears that Rackham consciously set out to establish a repertoire of compositional devices by which he could fit his vignette style into the frame required by book publishers. A sign that he was consciously aware of the need for composition in his work may be taken from the compositions of the illustrations to his early books, such as *Rip van Winkle* and *Alice in Wonderland*, which he constructed with more care than he did the later ones. Despite all the devices he adopted, there are examples of work in which the compositions simply do not hold together, and very many of Rackham's colour plates are little more than loose-edged unframed illustrations which have been dropped into a compositional square: this is especially true of his illustrations to Poe's *Tales of Mystery and Imagination*, 1935, which is evidence that Rackham never fully integrated the compositional aspect into his art form. In cases such as the picture of the commander of the little men of the Catskill mountains, which was first a line drawing (figure 52), and then a full-colour plate (figure 41)

52 Original pen drawing. The gentleman on his side, at the bottom,
is a preparatory drawing for plate 41

Rackham went to great inventive lengths to structure the image harmoniously
and satisfactorily into the frame (see page 75), but at other times there is a lack
of cohesion, and the plate remains merely a coloured, ragged-edged drawing
(figure 53). This latter effect, noted in the drawings for Poe, becomes more and

53 'The death of Aase', *Peer Gynt* 1936

more common in the later books, when we may presume that Rackham felt that he need not make as much effort: in *Peer Gynt*, of 1936, for example, no fewer than six of the twelve colour plates are quite obviously ragged-edged vignette drawings dropped into the picture frame rectangle.

We may trace in Rackham's illustrations six quite distinct compositional devices by which he sought to give structure to his images. The first of these we may call the 'close-up' technique, for this involves the idea of filling his picture space with one compelling image, and then structuring this image into the frame with relatively uninteresting, virtually abstract, elements. A fine example of this is the image of the three Catskills seated in the roots of a tree (figure 54).

54 'They maintained the gravest faces', *Rip van Winkle* 1905

55  Illustration from 'Stories of the Table Round' in *Little Folks* 1902

The second technique is derived from certain compositional tendencies within *art nouveau*, ultimately from the Japanese print's influence on French painting. In this, the pictorial elements are gathered in the upper part of the picture leaving a fairly empty, or even totally empty, foreground, usually with some central figure breaking the horizontal line, and thus joining together the upper and lower divisions. We find this in 'His likeness on their New Year Cakes' (figure 39). The printing requirements for some of the illustrations for *Little Folks* may have awakened Rackham's interest in this compositional device, for the two-colour roller printing method required that the artist make a compositional division of the pictorial space into two distinct areas, which would allow the colours to be printed at the same time, yet without coming into contact with each other (see figure 55). The ingenuity which this demanded of Rackham

69

56 'As he moves slowly away, Wotan turns and looks sorrowfully back at
Brünnhilde', *The Rhinegold and the Valkyrie* 1910

must have been sufficient to open his eyes to the possibility of contrasting space
against pictorial elements.

The third device restricts the interest to the lower half of the frame (figure 56).
Since this tends to involve a low vantage point of view for the spectator, it is a
device most frequently used by Rackham in illustrations to epic stories, or in
actions in which the reader is required to consider the actions depicted on a higher
level of being than normal, the empty space above the action suggesting
spirituality or the 'domain of the gods' depending upon the context of the story.
It is not surprising that no fewer than five of the plates in the epic *Siegfried and
the Twilight of the Gods* of 1911 adopts this technique, for it is found in 'Mime at
the Anvil', 'Brunnhilde throws herself into Siegfried's arms·, 'The Three Norns',

'The Ravens of Wotan', and 'Siegfried's death'. Rackham is fond of giving a low vantage point for his gnarled or anthropomorphized trees—the picture of Rip's ragged and wild children, and the tree (figure 57) is typical of this kind of composition, though it does not fall into the third category of compositional devices.

The fourth compositional structure is based on the inverted triangle, which has its apex in the lower part of the pictorial area, and its base near the top.

57 'His children were as ragged and wild as if they belonged to nobody', *Rip van Winkle* 1905

Two fine examples of this ingenious structure may be seen in the composition which shows the cow in the cabbage patch, from *Rip van Winkle*, (figure 58) and in the delicious image of Alice's swimming companions (figure 59). The triangle inverted in this way is an especially useful compositional device in illustrations which are intended to convey movement, for the inverted triangle is itself off balance, and therefore conveys a sense of unrest to the spectator.

58  'His cow would go astray or get among the cabbages', *Rip van Winkle* 1905

59 'The Pool of Tears', *Alice's Adventures in Wonderland* 1907

The fifth compositional device is almost a classical one, for it is involved with structuring one of the main participants of the action into the side of the picture, thus giving a firm anchorage for the entire illustration. Rackham is especially fond of anchoring a group of people (figure 85) in this way, so as to leave an interesting vignette pattern of interlaced shapes, which are none the less firmly tied to the straight edge of the frame.

60 'Freia, the fair one', *The Rhinegold and The Valkyrie* 1910

Rackham used the sixth compositional device only rarely, but he employs it to great effect: the composition is divided vertically which adds a strong feeling of dignity to the scene. The tendency is for Rackham to choose a figure, centralize this near or on the frame base, and then to structure this into the top of the frame, the whole action or figure being contained in a vertical slab within the composition. Two fine examples of this type of composition may be found in *Siegfried*: the picture of Brunnhilde kissing the ring which Siegfried has left

74

with her (figure 62), and an even more free example in the exquisite image of
the three Rhinemaidens (figure 61) joined in an interplay of *art nouveau* ripples
to one another at the base, and structured at the top by the roots of a tree trunk.

Compositional devices take time and considerable thought, as well as an
alert sensitivity to the requirements of the story. It is probably for this reason
that the compositions of the plates in Rackham's earlier books are generally
better than in the later, in which he tends to fall back on the relatively easy
compositional device of simply dropping in rough-edged vignettes into frames,

61 'Siegfried! Siegfried! Our warning is true. Flee, oh flee from the curse!'
*Siegfried and the Twilight of the Gods* 1911

62 'Brünnhilde kisses the ring that Siegfried has left with her',
*Siegfried and The Twilight of the Gods* 1911

or of framing images which might as well have been left as vignettes, for as his
fame grew so did the demand on his time.

A survey of an artist's technique and compositional method which ignores
the imaginative use of pictorial elements employed by the artist would be
unsatisfactory. In Rackham's case, the imaginative element is so important that
it must be accorded a separate study within the next chapter. However, the
best of his illustrations are such a perfect combination of technique, compositional structure and imaginative sensibility, that ultimately each plate must
be examined from the point of view of how those three elements combine as a
whole.

# Rackham's Imagination

I N HIS refreshing autobiography *Surprised by Joy*, C. S. Lewis writes about
the time when he 'fell deeply under the spell of Dwarfs—the old bright-
hooded, snowly-bearded dwarfs we had in those days before Arthur Rackham
sublimed, or Walt Disney vulgarized, the earthmen. I visualized them so intensely
that I came to the very frontier of hallucination; once, walking in the garden,
I was for a second not quite sure that a little man had not run past me into the
shrubbery.' Lewis was describing a period of his childhood around 1910, and so
for once he was wrong in his sense of history, for by that time Rackham had
produced the best of his earthmen, and was already recognized as essentially
the artist of fantasy. However, Lewis was accurate in his imaginative grasp of
the extent to which artists such as Rackham and Walt Disney (himself clearly
influenced by the English artist) were responsible for creating the fairy world
for the coming generations. In this reminiscence from Lewis we may see a concept
of the function of art which reaches into the very fundamentals of our being.

It has been said that Rackham invented a new type of child, but the truth
is more subtle than this—Rackham invented a new kind of reality. Whilst he
obviously created a fairy world on paper, it is also true that he created a fairy
world in the imagination of thousands and perhaps millions of people, and yet
it may be considered 'tedious' or 'academically unsound' to ask whether Rackham
believed in the fairy world he created. As we have seen, the external world of
Rackham, and his intellectual statements about his work (he wrote in 1934,
'. . . I firmly believe in the greatest stimulating and educative power of the
imaginative, fantastic, and playful pictures and writings for children in their
most impressionable year . . .'), were very far removed from his inner imaginative
grasp, and so we must separate the imaginative artist from what he said about
his art form. In a sense, if Rackham could draw fairies, then they must exist,
although questions about the reality of fairies, are 'on the very frontier of
hallucination', those domains which the ancient cartographers would prefer not
to explore, but would simply scrawl on their maps, 'here there be dragons',
challenging further exploration with fear.

Quiller-Couch, who was rash enough to touch upon the subject in his
introduction to Rackham's *Book of Pictures*, said that if the fairies do not exist

then the children would have to invent them. We would wish to take the matter one step further, with the reflection that if fairies did not exist, then children would not exist either. Illustrations and fairy stories enrich then vivify the soul almost to the extent that television destroys the soul, and the contribution which a fairy-story writer or illustrator such as Rackham makes to the development of the human soul is too vast to be accounted for. One may not within the scope of one lifetime alone draw up a balance sheet of merit and demerit within the sphere of art, since all creativity spreads out into the future, sets its tone, and also spreads back into the past, and revitalizes it. This is why art and the development of the imaginative faculty are so vital, for it is only through the arts and allied developments that our soul-life may retain contact with the evolving strains of civilization. Art is involved with the magic which maintains the perception and soul-life of humanity, and since it works this magic through the domain of the imagination, it is little understood, which is why the terms 'art' and 'imagination' have for some time been hidden under a debris of words, jargon and books. This expression of soul-life is frequently accounted almost as 'mere imagination', and it seems that there is no modern William Blake to shout the superficial pseudo-psychologists and art-theorists into silence.

It would be difficult to assess the contribution which Rackham made to the development of book illustration. As the high prices of his books and every popular sale of those monstrously large 'Rackham' prints indicate, he is firmly wedged in the public mind, and many people who otherwise know nothing of books and illustrations are fond of his work. Some bibliophiles (a type who likes to go against the tide, a healthy enough way of passing a lifetime) openly grouse at his books, and describe them as 'non-books', complaining at their de luxe effects, tissue covers, tipped-in plates and so on, whilst otherwise sensitive men bruit it about that his illustrations are 'insincere' or the offshoot of an adolescent mind. Fortunately, a real assessment of Rackham's contributions and merits brushes aside all such considerations as books, non-books and insincerity, for it is in the realm of the invisible that his true contribution has been the most powerful. Like all great artists, he has enriched the imagery and the imaginative grasp of his tribe and in so doing he has contributed to the vital growth of soul upon which culture depends. In this respect he is placed among the small group of artists to whom we owe homage, especially in this day and age when the very word 'soul' is scarcely understood, used reluctantly or imprecisely, and hardly mentioned without a certain embarrassment even in universities or art schools, once the last redoubts of our cultural defences. For all the beautiful and exciting drawing he has left behind, his real value is to be sensed in the invisible world of the spirit; it is to be felt, not seen, and yet by that glorious paradox which lies behind the artistic life, what is to be felt lies mainly in the seeing.

It is one of the functions of art for the artist to invent a new kind of perception. The artist does this by having the temerity and grace to point out something which should be seen, but which has not been seen before. Anyone who loves the work of Bonnard will not be able to look from a high window in a French house,

63 'Some say, no evil thing that walks by night . . . hath hurtful
power o'er true virginity', *Comus* 1921

without seeing through his eyes the street below; it is not possible to walk
through the countryside of England without seeing through the eyes of Constable,
any more than it is possible to free oneself of Cézanne when one reaches for an
apple on a plate. Within such a context, Rackham influenced our perception of
the world. We may see a curious tree, and point it out as being a Rackham tree,
by which we would probably mean that it is a 'humanized' tree (though it is
our mind which grants it that kind of life), yet the important thing is that if
Rackham had not lived and drawn, we might never have noticed the tree at all.

The artist adds to our stock of imagery, and enriches our visual perceptions,
and an artist of the calibre of Rackham adds images of a world slightly beyond
the familiar world of experience. Dicky Doyle will amuse us with his fairies,
but it is an artist of the calibre of Arthur Rackham who bewitches us into
expecting that our step might disturb a fairy funeral in the grass near the coast,
or that we might tread on a bespectacled elf with a face much like that of
Rackham, as we step over the tulips in Kensington Gardens (figure 38).

In fact, Rackham's imaginative strain represents the meeting of three
streams of artistic activity which have an ancient ancestry, all three of which

were clearly defined before the end of the nineteenth century. These may be summarized as being the humorous stream of book illustration, which found an important source in the piquant drolleries of Cruikshank, and the tragi-comic escapism of that lonely traveller, Edward Lear. Then there is the didactic stream, at its worst in the frightful schoolbook illustrations, at its best in the drawings for fables, or even in the moralizing enchantment of such an artist as E. V. Boyle in *The Story Without an End*. Thirdly, there is the stream which has its fount in the fairy world, populated in the late nineteenth century by creatures from the pen of Dicky Doyle and H. J. Ford, with a plethora of dragons, elves, sylphs and salamanders from a hundred and one books bought for children and often read by adults.

Rackham, almost by accident it would seem, brought together the three separate skeins of the cartoon, the fable and the fairy story, and wove these together in his own personal tapestry. In some respects Tenniel brought together the three streams also, especially in his illustrations for *Alice*. Unfortunately Sir John was even less than Rackham a colour-man—and even if he had been a colourist, then the lithographic processes and the wood-printing of the day would have made short shrift of flights of fancy. Infinite skill was required to produce delicate lithography from the weighty stones, and few of the colour woodblocks, save perhaps the best of the Leighton brothers or of Benjamin Fawcett, were produced to a standard which would have granted the ethereal quality Rackham demanded. Even Doyle's *In Fairyland*, printed by Evans with more care than he lavished in his later toy books, is heavy in comparison with even the worst of those artists who worked after the introduction of the four-colour process.

Rackham came just in time to bring together the three streams. He arrived, perhaps belated in view of early promise, just as the full technical power of four-colour process made the artist free, and he had the imaginative vision to take advantage of this freedom. The earlier four-colour work of Howard Pyle gave rise to compositions more exciting and dramatic than ever Rackham projected, but whilst Pyle constructed a style of his own, he never constructed a world of his own, as did Rackham. Rackham came to artistic maturity at the right time; he professed a dislike for the four-colour process, and certainly imposed his own will on the block-makers, but the process liberated him, and because he was able to use line and colour with technical freedom, he was in a better position than Tenniel or any of his graphic predecessors to pull together the cartoon, the fable and the fairy story into one coloured whole.

In the delightful editions of such popular magazines as *Little Folks* and *Cassell's Magazine* published around the end of the last century, we may find many examples of Rackham's drawings, and some intimation of the greatness to come (see previous chapter). More important than this, yet, is the work of other contributors who worked alongside Rackham, and in their own way represented one or other of the three streams which were to flow together through Rackham's pen. The cartoon style is best represented by the work of Harry Neilson, ribald and almost crude in his use of line, working in a style to which certain modern comics are still indebted. Along with Neilson, we may list Stewart Orr and Harry Rowntree. The fairy story in these magazines is best served by Rackham himself, though he is merely heading a well-established Victorian tradition. The delicate line drawings of Rainey have an individualistic touch which reminds one of Rackham, especially in the light handling of fairies.

We see from such drawings that Neilson, and indeed a whole host of Victorian draughtsmen who told animal moralities and fairy stories, portray their animals in clothing. Tenniel's White Rabbit could scarcely have worn only a watch without a waistcoat, and the illustrations to the so-called first children's book, by that remarkable Member of Parliament William Roscoe,* were given clothes by the youthful artist Mulready. Some of Dicky Doyle's animals wore trousers, scarves and capes, whilst his elves clearly disliked going nude. However, the important point is that, for all their human clothing, for all that they speak where necessary with human tongues, and point their morals with something verging on human gesture, these creatures always look like animals. Some of them, indeed, might, with a few deft alterations, or even merely without the clothes, find their place convincingly in the pages of a zoological guide. When Blacky the pig in H. J. Ford's drawing catches the big bad wolf and cooks him, he deigns to put on an apron, but otherwise, like his brothers and his mother, he is naked, quite recognizably a pig. When the fox takes hold of Blacky's unfortunate brother and trusses him for cooking, he does so with foxy paws: he remains in the illustration a fox, in much the same spirit as 'pigs is pigs'. It is only with Rackham that pigs become human beings.

Like his contemporaries and peers, Rackham sometimes decks his animals in clothing, not merely to introduce a human element, but actually to lend significant point to their personality, or to add humour to humour. Any artist may make an animal humorous by adding clothes—this is one of the oldest tricks in the trade—but few artists could make a sausage live by clothing it (figure 65).

*The Butterfly's Ball,* 1807, printed by John Harris

65 Illustration from 'The Mouse, the Bird and the Sausage',
*Fairy Tales of the Brothers Grimm* 1907

Rackham had a most remarkable talent for individualizing his human animals, sometimes through their clothing, but more often through their faces, and especially through their 'hands'. His anthropomorphizing is done not merely on the principle that animals are human, but on the further extension of that principle which holds that many humans are, in their soul-life, much like animals. In this humanizing tendency he was pulling together the two streams of the cartoon and the moralizing.

In his superb illustration of 'The Hare and Tortoise' from his *Aesop's Fables* (figure 49), we see the splendid gesture of the fox, arms folded in self-indulgent mockery, jauntily sporting a red coat which has the cheek to verge on the pink and style of the huntsman. His foxy face is more a character cartoon than it is a drawing of a fox: he is at once a fox, even an archetypal fox, and yet he is almost human in looks and in posture. Each of the six animals quietly mocking the tortoise resembles in many ways a human type more than an animal type. We all know these creatures which are to be found in almost any pub in our country. The dormouse is the perennial henpecked husband, scarf worn not for protection from the cold, but because the wife says he must wear a scarf, no doubt taken from the drawer marked 'scarves'. One suspects that he is enjoying the mocking of the tortoise because he is all too frequently the object of derision himself. The hare wears gloves not because hares wear gloves, but because this is precisely the smart-alec human type who invariably wears white gloves. One scarcely notices that this hare has *hands*. The stork against the wall also has hands, and we see immediately that he is the grouser, the morose and negative melancholic, stirred not into movement, or even to a smile, by the challenge of the tortoise; his weighty lethargy is overcome sufficiently for his eye muscle to be called into play. We have seen this stork before, too, leaning against the bar anywhere in the world, confident only when drinking himself into forgetfulness of the world which has so played him into bitterness through failing to see and appreciate his true worth.

The best of Rackham's types are human in animal vesture. In many respects they are a more benign equivalent of those drawings being produced in Germany at about the same time by the more virulent George Grosz, in a satire more relentless, but none the less geared to portraying human foibles in animal masks, on the principle that the human soul is best portrayed by its animal form. In essence there is little difference in the art which turns pride into a dandified and absurdly self-confident hare, and the art which turns sexual desire into a grunting pig-nosed man. The difference is merely that between love and hate— Rackham could put up with people, even loved them, whilst Grosz was ill at ease with the world in which he lived.

This remarkable ability to combine the human and the animal in one figure lies at the root of many of Rackham's fine pictures. His goblins are human (some of his humans are goblins—perhaps he sees no clear distinction between the devic world (see page 112) and the human plane), his animals are often merely human after all, and even his trees and shrubs are best described as humanoid. The division between imagination and reality in Rackham's world is a tenuous one, and because of this a new world is created. When Rackham chooses to draw an animal without his powerful anthropomorphizing, then, while he may produce a fine drawing, he usually fails to produce a work of art. The vignette from 'The Fox and the Grapes' (figure 66), which is within the text illustrated by plate 49, is a nice enough drawing, but it in no way approaches the genius of the humanized fox in 'The Hare and the Tortoise'. The difference between the two is not the difference between a small line vignette and a 'finished' colour plate: it is a difference in attitude. The vignette is ordinary, and might well have been drawn by a dozen artists of that time, but the fox of the colour plate could have been drawn only by Rackham.

The peculiar secret of Rackham's success in seizing upon the essence of the human and portraying it in animal form, which is after all the basic device of the morality, is unwittingly touched upon in Chesterton's delightful introduction to the 1912 edition of *Aesop's Fables*: 'There can be no good fable with human beings in it. There can be no good fairy tale without them.' Rackham's genius is such that it bridges the two, and carries the didactic fable into the realm of

66 'The Fox and the Grapes', *Aesop's Fables* 1912

# ÆSOP'S FABLES

## THE FOX AND THE GRAPES

A HUNGRY Fox saw some fine bunches of Grapes hanging from a vine that was trained along a high trellis, and did his best to reach them by jumping as high as he could into the air. But it was all in vain, for they were just out of reach: so he gave up trying, and walked away with an air of dignity and unconcern, remarking, " I thought those Grapes were ripe, but I see now they are quite sour."

fairy story, and lends to the imaginative world of fairies a tangible and convincing reality. Rackham succeeds in dispensing with the merely human (for the fox, the dormouse and the hare are clearly animals), and thus he remains in part with the fable. At the same time, he maintains a sufficient contact with the human (for the fox, the dormouse and the hare are also clearly human), and so retains the fairy story. Rackham's best illustrations of the kind combine the fable and the fairy world, and in so doing they add a new dimension to the books for which they were intended. To imagination he adds a heavy dose of hard visual reality, and to so-called reality he adds a heavy dose of imagination. This is surely one reason why the characters of fairies, gnomes and pixies in his numerous plates are more convincing proof of the existence of fairy land than the photographs of fairies and gnomes which were being taken in the north of England, even while he drew.* Reality is an aspect of imagination, and it requires a frequent injection of new imagination in order that it may find its own vitality and refreshment.

As Barbara Edwards, Rackham's daughter, relates, when Rackham first saw the photographs of fairies he said that they were forgeries, and quite clearly based on his own drawings. He resolved to write to Conan Doyle to this effect, but it is not certain that he did this. In all fairness to those who believed in the genuineness of the Cottingely photographs, it must be pointed out that there is no showing of 'forgery' if it can be established that the fairies did indeed resemble certain fairies created by Rackham. It was one of the tenets of those involved in the occult lore of fairies that these devic beings, who are normally invisible to ordinary sight, may manufacture a temporary body from a semi-materiality called elemental essence. However, it is possible for them to appear through this elemental essence only by taking a thought-form manufactured by human beings. The photographed fairy is, according to the occult explanation a meeting of an invisible and indeed formless creature with the thoughtform created by a human being. Since the thought forms of human beings are unconsciously derived from the stock of traditional images (which of course Rackham himself used, refined and slightly changed—thereby creating very strong thoughtforms) the fairies, and indeed all related elemental beings such as gnomes and salamanders, appear in a familiar guise, which in turn confirm the traditional image. It is difficult to see how fairies would appear otherwise than similar in appearance to those created by Rackham: they are both, so far as mere appearances are concerned, the product of the human mind.

With Rackham even the humans who dwell in his world must be rendered ethereal, not merely because like all humans they are princes and princesses in heavy disguise, but because they live in a supra-human world which is more real than our everyday dream. In this Martin Birmbaum is right in saying that Rackham is happier when he forsakes ordinary human habitations, for the paradise of children or magical realms not meant for mortal feet to tread: in fact,

*See E. L. Gardner *Fairies: the Story of the Cottingley Photographs.*

67 Drawing from *A Midsummer Night's Dream* 1908

there is really no 'ordinary human habitation' for one who sees the world aright, for everything is a mystery and a wonder. It is on this level, and upon this level alone, that Rackham's art may be described as being linked with the vision of childhood.

One of the most illuminating ways in which it is possible to study the influence of Rackham's imaginative grasp on book illustration is to make a comparison between his drawings for a particular text, and a set of earlier drawings for that same text. An instructive comparison may be made between Rackham's drawings for *Rip van Winkle* and some of the better earlier illustrations, for it is Rackham's images for this text that define particularly well his penchant for passages which give free vent to imaginative interpretation.

Washington Irving gives fairly specific descriptions of the strange men Rip meets in the Catskill mountains: they are 'odd looking personages' dressing in 'quaint outlandish fashion'; they have peculiar visages, 'the face of one seemed to consist entirely of nose', and so on, whilst all the company sported beards, the entire group reminding Rip of the figures in an old Flemish painting. When the Victorian artist Gordon Brown illustrated this text in 1887, he took Irving at his word, and presented them as ordinary, if outlandish, persons wearing costumes of a bygone Flemish age. Darley, who illustrated *Rip van Winkle* in the 1894 J. M. Dent edition of the *Sketch-Book*, refrained from picturing the little men at all, but concentrated on Rip's laziness and penchant for gossip. In this way, paragraphs which so fascinated Rackham, and which now fascinate us, were left blank of all illustration. The postscript, which as we shall see, Rackham plays with outrageously by stirring up with his pen a new world of imaginary beasties that exceed even Irving's Catskill, was illustrated by William Hart in a melancholic little wood-engraving which might well be a picture of any lakeside scene more appropriate to Wordsworth's heaviest excursions than to Knickerbocker. An examination of these drawings, with which Rackham would of necessity have been familiar (some of the Darleys were used alongside those of Rackham in the early *Sketchbook*), reveals something of the impact which Rackham's imaginative vision must have had on his contemporaries.

68 'The Kaatsberg or Catskill mountains have always been a region full
of fable.' *Rip van Winkle*, 1905

It is left to the imagination and pen of Rackham to persuade us that these
men are not human, but small creatures much like gnomes (figure 92). Irving
had described the first of this strange horde as 'a short square-built old fellow',
but they were otherwise presented as rather strange humans, related to the
early Flemish settlers. Such has been Rackman's influence that it is difficult for
our own generation to think of these men as other than belonging to the fairy
world, or to a world of nature sprites—grotesque humanoids at worst, earthmen-
gnomes at the best—yet Irving at no point described them in such terms.

The realm of fantasy once entered into, Rackham was scarcely held to such
matters as nuances of the text, and he flung himself into a spree of imagination
which fortunately ends to our advantage in the majority of plates. His portrayal
of the 'commander' of the group (figure 41) is more or less accurate to the text,

so far as the text goes, but the figure would stand as a delightful piece of drawing even as an isolated vignette, which is precisely what it was in an earlier edition. Rackham structures this line vignette into the frame with a stroke of genius. He is required to make the fellow small, yet to suggest at the same time that he was imposing, since he is the commander of the troupe. He does this by introducing a bevy of birds by which it is possible to gauge the approximate size. This is not in itself an original graphic device, but the manner in which he does it is extremely clever. Across the top of the plate he runs a branch, which echoes the horizontal of the frame, and thus aids the compositional effect: on this branch he perches four very anthropomorphic birds, one of which wears shoes. At one end of the branch he places a frowsy mother hen on her nest, knitting a sock. The imposing chief is thus placed fairly and squarely in an imaginative world well out of the range envisaged by Washington Irving, yet the picture remains true to the announced details of the text. The sensitive placing of the branch, of the hanging ball of wool, and this little entry into the absurd fable world which with Rackham is akin to the fairy realm, both places the commander in quite a different world to Rip, and at the same time transforms an original vignette line drawing into a well thought-out and beautifully designed frame.

The postscript to *Rip van Winkle*, supposedly from a memorandum of Knickerbocker, begins with the comment: 'The Kaatsberg or Catskill Mountains have always been a region of fable.' This gave us Hart's uninspired Wordsworthian image, but for Rackham it is an open invitation to people his frame with strange and exotic creatures, a vigorous image of three grotesqueries (figure 68). However, it seems that Rackham could not stop there, and in the same book he gives another version of the line, misquoting with 'The Kaatskill mountains had always been haunted by strange beings,' to accommodate a new vision of that fabulous world, this time in a night scene, with a variety of gnome-like creatures, and a few rather sinister flying beasties.* Rackham is not content with merely rendering the story more mysterious than the author suggested, but plunges Rip into a grotesque fairy land which Irving might have imagined, but certainly never penned. Rackham seems to have invoked a kind of draughts-

---

* In fact the misquote is that given for fig 68, since the postscript for which this plate is an illustration does not appear in the 1905 edition. Further complication arises because the illustrations are not in sequence.

69  Detail from fig 94

70 'Stand away from the window, please, madam; you're obstructing the other passengers!' *The Wind in the Willows* 1940

man's licence with a courage and ability which later he rarely emulated, and he over-illustrates, misquotes and generally renders mysterious, that our own clamour for fantasy might be quieted, and a new dimension be added to the American author's vision.

For all his imaginative propensity, Rackham produced illustrations which are remarkable for the degree to which they depart from the text, yet at the same time he rarely openly contradicts the letter of the text. His illustrations are frequently contiguous to the text, are commentaries on rather than illustrations to the text in the ordinary sense of the term. A good example of this is in the illustration of Rip s uncomfortable marital bed (figure 94), which shows in attendance a horde of laughing mice and jubilant spirits, though there is no mention of these in the literary version of the story. Other examples would not be hard to find, for it is Rackham's way to extend the narrative into another, more rarified dimension of imagination.

88

Yet in spite of these leaps from exactitude into imaginative fantasy, Rackham rarely makes a mistake, commits an irrelevance to the text, slips in chronology, or misses in a sequence of illustration, all common enough lapses with over-worked illustrators. A few examples do survive—Toad of Toad Hall changes size relative to humans (figure 70)—perhaps forgivable enough in a fairy story, but not so in a text with such a strong and delightfully fresh moral tone. In the 1909 *Gulliver's Travels* there are one or two slight slips of this kind. For example, to judge from the number of buttons on Gulliver's coat front (about six in the frontispiece in which he releases himself from the string, about twelve in the scene where he reviews the troops of Lilliput, and from the absence of pocket buttons in this latter picture and then the presence of two such buttons in the scene where he is being measured—figure 72), we might reasonably assume that he had two coats with him. However, this would contradict the text, which quite specifically has him washed ashore with only one set of clothing. A more serious graphic slip is that in the frontispiece the Lilliputians are dressed in European medieval garb, whilst in the scene showing the tailors measuring him for a new suit of clothing, the Lilliputians are dressed in semi-oriental garb. Perhaps this is what may be expected of an artist who is required to work at

71 'Gulliver released from the strings raises and stretches himself', *Gulliver's Travels* 1909

72 'The Lilliputian Tailors measure Gulliver for a new
suit of clothes', *Gulliver's Travels* 1909

wide intervals in the preparation of pictures between editions: the frontispiece
is dated 1909, whilst the tailor scene is dated 1904.

It is, indeed, surprising that Rackham did not fantasize completely in the
illustrations for Swift, and whilst there are some reasons why he did not portray
Gulliver's adventures in a more or less fantastic realm, it may be admitted that
for all Swift's sense of ordinary reportage, which is part and parcel of the voyage
genre of which the Gulliver account pretended to belong, the underlying sense
of fantasy (such as tiny men, giants, talking horses and degenerate gnomes)
could easily have lent itself to a more fantastic manner of interpretation. One

reason is that Swift, for his satire to work, really needed the book to hinge on 'ordinary' reality. However, this original reason was virtually invalid by the time Rackham set to work on the text, for much of Swift's satire and esoteric reference was lost to all but scholars, yet Rackham was following a 'graphic tradition' by which a pattern was set, with conventions of imagery which had to be followed. Perhaps the most compelling reason, however, was that the later drawings, although executed after Rackham's fantasy had reached its perfection, were to follow in style and spirit the drawings of the earliest (1900) edition of the title, which were worked before Rackham had achieved his confident style of fantasy. It is a tribute to Swift's style, and to the tradition of graphic reportage which generations of illustrators had built around the book, that Rackham did not depart more rigorously into a quaint, fantastic Rack-hamerie. A few years later, John Hassell in his version projected Gulliver into a more imaginative burlesque, but in so doing portrayed a whimsical world which lost the mordant force of the original Swift.

A more obvious example of a graphic lapse is to be found in *Rip van Winkle*, for in Rip's sleep or drunken drowse, twenty years have passed, and Washington Irving drily tells us that the accustomed phlegm and drowsy tranquility of the village has given rise to a busy, bustling, disputatious tone. With Washington Irving, this is no doubt a jibe against the increase in bureaucracy since the liberation from 'King and Country', but what concerns Rackham is the change, not the reasons for the change, so in this matter he follows the text. The inn has changed, and with it the inn sign as the amusing text requires, the well-kept Dutch inn under the patronage of the King has given way to a rickety shambles under the sign of George Washington. Rackham remembers this in the two

73 Detail from fig. 72

74 'They crowded round him, eyeing him from head to foot with great
curiosity', *Rip van Winkle* 1905

drawings but he forgets to replace the large trees of the earlier state with the
flag pole which should sport the stars and stripes (figure 74).

Whilst Rackham is rarely open to a valid charge of lapse or mistake in his
illustration, he is only too often legitimately open to a charge of irrelevance.
Indeed, many of his finest illustrations are, from a literary point of view, quite
irrelevant to the text, and in some cases it is only the beauty of the illustration,
the quality of the artwork, or the fantasy of the concept, which permits the
illustration room within the book at all. Surely there can be no finer irrelevance
than the illustration to 'Certain biscuit-bakers have gone so far as to impress
his likeness on their New-Year Cakes' (a passage which is a semi-aside to the

92

text in any case), for which Rackham produced the snow idyll of figure 39. Only Rackham would have illustrated the text in this way; indeed, only Rackham would have chosen to illustrate that line at all, in a book with so many throw-away gifts to the imaginative artist.

The most magnificent of Rackham's irrelevances are what we might call 'marginalia', as they are in a sense an offshoot of the medieval tendency which finds scribes and illuminators doodling in the margins of their vellum sheets, and carefully adding irrelevant creatures, beasties and humans in their initial letters and scrollwork. Some of Rackham's illustrations are irrelevant, and merely an excuse for the exercise of the neo-gothic pen, but his marginalia, like the tail-pieces of Bewick, are always irrelevant, and almost by virtue of their textual irrelevance deepen the imaginative impact and scope of the illustrations. The marginalia became a delightful tool by which Rackham might push his love for the gothic and for the minutiae of the fairy world to extremes: the irrelevance and irreverence is carried to such an absurd extent that they cannot be ignored. An outstanding example of this kind of irrelevance has already been noted in figure 94, an illustration which shows Rip van Winkle in 'the fiery furnace of domestic tribulation'. Rackham has neatly ignored the fact that the couple are, so far as the story is concerned, living in abject poverty due to Rip's aversion to profitable labour: the bed is distinctly upper middle class and beautifully curtained. We may expect a poor home to have mice, but not such a motley crew of goblins—and certainly Washington Irving never mentions them in his text. Perhaps Rackham is merely reminding us that goblins and spirits are 'around' in that valley, if not actually visible, though his tendency towards irrelevance normally does not require excuse for plaguing houses, forests, trees and bed companions in this way.

The host of goblins around, above and under the bed, may well be so much graphic tomfoolery, intended to create a link between the Catskill mountains and the village, or perhaps to express the bad thought-forms of the termagent wife—and to Rackham a straight-forward picture of a nagging wife in bed would not offer much by way of visual amusement. The two delicious enactments in the foreground entirely escape artistic licence, however, and with these we have unadulterated examples of Rackhamesque marginalia. The goblin standing in Rip's slippers is obviously a goblin amusing himself greatly by listening to what is being said, and observing what is being done, or not being done, in that bed; at the same time he is also Rip's *alter ego* (quite literally standing in Rip's shoes), convulsed with the compensating laughter of self-mockery. Similar forms are the two mice, lost in rolling laughter either at Rip, or at Arthur Rackham, his name clearly set out on that scroll of 1905 around which they frolic. Perhaps we have here the artist gently mocking himself, after two years of marriage, or even laughing at Everyman; it could be that there are such goblins and mice in every bedroom.

In *English Fairy Tales* (1918) Rackham resists the obvious temptation to clothe and anthropomorphize the three bears, and the added comment in the

75 Vignette used first in the Haddon Hall
series 1899 onwards, and in several
subsequent Dent publications.

illustrations depends upon the details which place them in a human middle-class setting. The porridge bowls are of good quality, nicely designed, and on the wall, a Dégas ballet dancer, a French eighteenth-century print or painting, and to the right a Dutch oil picture. This is subtle marginalia which reflects on the social status of the three bears, and adds amusement to the drawing.

Such marginalia abound in Rackham, and form half the delight of his work, though it is true that one must develop an eye to rightly appreciate them. For example, who is the bewigged eighteenth-century gent listening to the intimately conversational Catskill creature in the region of fable (figure 68)? Already the imagination begins to weave a story around his curious and unexpected presence in these mountains. Why in the same picture does the disconsolate gnome sit so glum, and why has he hung his right shoe on the tree? Perhaps there is no answer to such questions—certainly one will find no answer in the text—and such marginalia are merely opportunities for the imagination to take a free ride, in that state so loved by Irving himself, 'when a man can be idle with impunity'—a question not of time, but of inner estate.

76 Vignette used first in the Haddon Hall
series 1899 onwards, and in several
subsequent Dent publications

# RACKHAM'S IMAGINATION

It is not possible to touch upon Rackham's marginalia and irrelevancies without thinking specifically of his tail-pieces and head-pieces, which for the most part have nothing to do with the texts they adorn. The most interesting of the early vignettes appeared at a curious time in Rackham's career when he produced a series of delicate 'rustic' drawings which are in many ways among the finest of his non-fantasy drawings of the previous century (figure 75). These first appeared in Dewar's *Wild Life in Hampshire* in 1899. Although the book was officially, and indeed delightfully, illustrated by R. W. A. Rouse and Ralph Hodgson, Rackham contributed eleven chapter headings, six tail-piece vignettes and the endpapers, most of which were to be used again and again in many books produced by J. M. Dent in the next few years, sometimes in the most unlikely places; for example, the same heading which was used for a chapter on countryside creatures appears as a heading for 'Much Ado About Nothing' in the 1909 edition of *Tales from Shakespeare*. Most of these drawings have a freshness of vision, an exciting quality of line, and a texture well suited to the hand-made paper in which the Haddon Hall Library series were printed with their very English titles, *Hunting, Shooting* and *Fishing*. In these drawings appears the freshness of a new decorative feeling, which emerges in Rackham's work periodically, and a capacity for natural illustration which he never surpassed in later years without the use of colour.

77 Vignette used first in the Haddon Hall
series 1899 onwards, and in several
subsequent Dent publications

What is important to our theme is that it is in this book that Rackham establishes himself as the artist who is prepared to use quite irrelevant goblins as the subjects for tail-pieces for texts which find no mention of goblins, or indeed of any realm other than the English sensible world of appearances. Rackham in one case feebly justifies their presence at the foot of a chapter on butterflies (figure 77) by giving them wings, though these are much too puny to fly with. A second goblin tail-piece (figure 78) has scarcely any justification, however, and we see that Rackham intended the irrelevance—a portent for the future.

78 Vignette used first in the Haddon Hall
series 1899 onwards, and in several
subsequent Dent publications

With Rackham as with that other artist-craftsman of a hundred years earlier, Thomas Bewick, one has the impression that it might be possible to write a full appreciation and detailed biography of both, with reference only to the vignette tail-pieces and chapter headings, so important a reflection are these of the style, temperament, beliefs and developments of the two men. From the tail-pieces Rackham was one with Bewick in his approach to nature, whilst for both the irrelevances were the true inspiration. For Bewick, the true personal delight was for him to show a fisherman urinating, a hog-tied dog waiting to drown with the rising tide, a portrait of a fly in large, or an egotistical glance at his own thumb's papillary ridges—all admittedly asides to the real meat of the book, but asides which are remembered more completely than the actual illustrations. So it is with Rackham, though his irrelevances carry us into the land of fairies and goblins, rather than into Newcastle and Northumbrian farmyards. But the interesting thing is that the presence of these beings in books of a more ordinary subject suggest, almost casually, a contiguous evolutionary stream of nature spirits alongside that of animals, plants and man. Rackham, for the first time, and certainly not for the last time, will present one tail-piece as a mouse (figure 76), the next as a goblin, tacitly asking 'after all, what is the difference, for are they not both parts of nature?' When Quiller-Couch in his introduction to Rackham's *Book of Pictures* gave his opinion on the artist, he was constrained to say of the drawings in the book that 'as they were not invented to order, to serve some other fellow's imagination—prove that he does his spiriting *con amore* and with belief in it'.* *With love*, perhaps, and the love shows in the vision of nature just as much as in the vision of faerie.

One unfortunate day some psychologist will emerge to submit Rackham's symbols and marginalia to scrutiny, to that superficial play with symbols which

* Actually, Quiller-Couch didn't appear to be aware of the histories of the pictures he was writing about: the sadness is that almost without exception they were in fact invented to 'serve some other fellow's imagination'. However, Sir Arthur was not to know that, and in any case, his conclusion is still just, even when stripped of its argument.

79 'The Indians considered them the abode of the spirits',
*Rip van Winkle* 1905

is based on an absurd concept of an intelligent subconscious activity in man, and we shall learn something about Rackham, much about the psychologist, and nothing at all about the imagination by which Rackham was served. We would see what could not be written in all high seriousness about the bewigged and worried gentlemen lost in the Catskills, about the old man in the tail-piece vignette who is holding the hands of two young children, and about the strange artist who draws goblins into books on natural history, and who is not afraid to portray himself so frequently in the outward guise of gnomes, fairies or birds. However, until such an analysis, let us join with Rackham in his unspoken but frequently painted axiom, that reality is an aspect of imagination, rather than imagination being merely an aspect of reality.

# RACKHAM'S BEST BOOK
# ILLUSTRATIONS I

## From *Two Old Ladies* to de luxe *Peter Pan*

MANY of the more sophisticated books published under Rackham's name were nominally for children, in that they had titles loved by children, and fairy-story themes. In reality, however, the majority of these books were what we would now call 'coffee-table books', intended for those who, as Gleeson White put it at the end of the last century, 'babble of Botticelli, and profess to disdain any picture not conceived with "high art" mannerism'.* Indeed, they were not even intended for coffee tables, but to be locked securely in glass-fronted book-cases, away from sticky fingers and people who like to read. Even worse, some of the de luxe editions were clearly intended as investments, collected by collectors for collectors—and to judge from the prices nowadays, they were investments which have paid off well.

The gold-blocked calf-binding, the tissue-screened images† tipped on brown card—even though tissue screening was quite unnecessary—the pages hard to turn, the text often hard to read comfortably—all this is a long way from the innocent enjoyment offered by the very early books of Rackham, when he drew pictures for children's papers and for women's magazines which would surely have been thumbed to death.‡ 'Children', concluded Gleeson White, 'love picture-books, not as bibliophiles would consider wisely, but too well.' It may be argued as a tribute to Rackham that the adults should seek to protect his images from the children who certainly like his work, but who are generally philistine in regard to the pictures which illustrate their books. Anyone can draw for children, but few men can create a world of their own in which children and adults feel comfortable and entertained. It would be quite fatuous to suggest that any of Rackham's pictures were produced purely for children, after his fame set in with *Rip van Winkle*. After this time, his books were produced for a specific market which required a particular sensitivity, a special

---

* 'Children's Books and Their Illustrators' *The Studio* 1887–8.
†The tissue screening was quite unnecessary, a hangover from the lithographic plates for which screening had been necessary.
‡These early magazines with Rackham's illustrations may still be obtained at reasonable prices which is more than can be said for his well-known books. Some of the de luxe editions now fetch up to £100 ($250) whilst it is still possible to buy a bound series of *Cassell's Magazine* for as little as 75p ($2) in the right quarters.

private vision, a unique gothic flavour, in a word, a Rackhamerie which marks a permissive state of escapism, not into childhood but into a realm of adult fantasy to which all children are, by definition, strangers.

In comparison with the heavy de luxe investments, some of Rackham's early books are a joy to handle, especially those which were reprints of stories and illustrations from magazines. In this category come the *Two Old Ladies* and the *Zankiwank*, and it is hard to say which of these may be regarded as the first genuine 'Rackham'. In some respects, the *Two Old Ladies, Two Foolish Fairies and a Tom Cat* of 1897 may be taken as the earliest book in a style which we would not recognize as being Rackham's. The frontispiece, from which the beautiful gold blocking of the binding is derived, we have already noted as the earliest example of Rackham in full colour, and the quality of line within the book shows his work maturing both in sense of style and feeling for composition. The lively quality of this frontispiece (figure 23) is entirely lacking in the three other colour plates within this book, however, which are insipid, presumably because the themes he illustrated did not excite his fantasy. Some of the twenty-one line illustrations are interesting, as might be expected of the magazine provenance. (For a detailed survey of Rackham's early magazine illustrations which later appear in book form, see Appendix B, on page 183 above.) The farmer picking the flower fairies (figure 80) is an especially fine Rackham, with a lovely variety of line treatment.

80 'The farmer stooped again', *Two Old Ladies, Two Foolish Fairies, and a Tom Cat*, 1897

81 'At the gates of Shadowland', *The Zankiwank and the Bletherwitch* 1896

It is, however, with the illustrations for *The Zankiwank and the Bletherwitch* that the true Rackham fantasy begins to emerge consistently, and this might well be called the first good Rackham. Even the subtitle of this book augurs well for Rackham, as it is described as 'An Original Fantastic Fairy Extravaganza', and as the Rackham titlepage demonstrates, there is almost no limit to how extravagant the illustrator might be (figure 82). There is no colour in this book, but its forty line illustrations reveal a new Rackham to the world, one who is rarely tethered by borders, as with the *Two Old Ladies*, so that this neo-gothic feeling for line and space and for the integrity of pure surface finds a satisfying outlet, from the view of Topsy Turvey Land (figure 82) to the gates of Shadow Land, with Maude and Willie in the arms of the Zankiwank (figure 81). It is in this book that we find the first clear intimations that trees are really human beings, and in the delightful picture showing the Zankiwank sticking together the folks of the Secret Cavern and Topsy Turvey Land (and sticking the wrong bits to the wrong people), Rackham is moving towards his own fantastic style (figure 147). The text of Fitzgerald is good, the illustrations well matched to it, and it seems prophetic of Rackham's genius that the publishers or author should choose to preface the book with the words of Ruskin that might well be taken as Rackham's message in short: 'Imagination is always the ruling and divine power, and the rest of man is only the instrument which it sounds, or the tablet on which it writes.'

Some of the drawings produced in *Little Folks* between 1896 and 1905 rank among the best of Rackham's work, for the finest of them have an innocence of style, a freshness of vision, and feeling for humour and fantasy which was in some respects lost under the self-awareness of the recognized official 'Rackham style' which tended to become something of a weight on Rackham in later years.

82 Title page of *The Zankiwank and the Bletherwitch* 1896

It would be quite accurate to say that it was through his dealings with *Little Folks* that Rackham found himself, discovered his real metier to be line, his realm fairy land, his incentive force to be fantasy, and his love to be moved by humour. The importance of *Little Folks* to Rackham's career and reputation may only be fully grasped when we understand that it was the reprinting of these stories and pictures in book form which first announced to the general public the existence of a good quality illustrator of fantasy, and paved the way for those books such as *Rip van Winkle*, which brought Rackham real fame.

Before these books of light fantasy appeared on the market, however, Rackham had already illustrated several titles which are now much sought after by collectors, but which would probably be forgotten had they been illustrated by another hand. These books are largely in the 'journalistic' style, which showed much linear control and versatility, but little of the genius which was to flower in the next century. The appearance of *The Dolly Dialogues* and *Sunrise-Land* in 1894 reveals a graphic problem with which Rackham struggled for the best part of a decade, and to judge from the results, it appears to have been an unsuccessful struggle. The two styles of illustration in these books are so totally different that one might suppose, had they not been signed, that they were by two different artists. They must have been drawn and painted so differently because the publishers had required different techniques for their illustrations. The four pictures in *The Dolly Dialogues* are in the semi-photographic style (figure 83), in heavy line and wash, and they are to say the least, uninspired pictures.

The illustrations in *Sunrise-Land* are of an altogether lighter quality, and although they are based on photographs, they show little sign of this influence, and are in a fresh, fluent line, more evocative of the open air than of the box camera. It is immediately clear from a comparison of these early books that heavy wash is not in Rackham's blood, and that line is his proper outlet. The total failure of the early 'photographic wash' books is something of a surprise, since it is evident from some of his early water-colours that he liked working in wash, yet we find comparative failures in *The Sketchbook* up to *The Peradventures of Private Pagett*, and in this muddy stream of inferior wash are titles which would certainly have promised better had pure line been allowed. As it is, Washington Irving's *Tales of a Traveller* (1895) and the collective work *Brains and Bravery* (1903) and Cholmondeley's *Red Pottage* (1904) are all dreary in visualization, rather turgid in execution. It is almost inconceivable that Rackham should be producing work of this quality alongside the distinctive linear grotesqueries unless the exigencies of the freelance market and Rackham's own difficult economic situation at that time are taken into account. We might further explain these constant failures by suggesting that the publishers required such 'photographic wash' almost by tradition to illustrate texts relevant to 'real' situations and 'real' people. For all its stark unimaginativeness, the style was associated with adventure stories, in which the publishers would probably have used photographs themselves, had this been practical at the time.

83 '"I'm not going to tell you anything more",
said Miss Phyllis', *The Dolly Dialogues* 1894

The illustrations for *Two Old Ladies* were not the only ones originally published in *Little Folks* to take on a book form. Rackham's drawings for a group of series in this magazine* were published together in *The Land of Enchantment* in 1907. Many of these *Little Folks* originals were published in three colours: over the black of the letterpress two different colours were rolled, from a single divided roller. An example of this printing technique may be seen in figure 85, from the original *Little Folks* illustration to Lincoln's 'Stories of the Table Round', later published in much smaller format and uncoloured as one of the pictures in A. L. Haydon's *Stories of King Arthur* in 1910. The top of the drawing, including the dresses, faces and hands of those standing behind Galahad, as well as the apples, the castle turrets, the arms, face and doublet of the hero, is printed in orange. The lower part of the drawing, including the water, the chain and the hose-stocking of Galahad, is printed in blue. The space between the rollers would of course leave a white gap in the colour of the illustrations, and in this plate it is accommodated by Rackham leaving the

* These were B. S. Woolf's 'Harry and Herodotus' series, E. S. Buchheim's 'Stories from the Edda', and A. E. Bonser's two series 'The Maker of Ghosts and the Maker of Shadows' and 'The Stories of Ben the Sailorman'.

84 Full page cartoon from *Punch Almanack* for 1905

stone, the sword, the wooden post, the cobbles, Galahad's knee and the hem of his doublet uncoloured. Clearly, since Rackham would have been informed of the printing technique envisaged for these series of *Little Folks* drawings, the nature of his composition and design would be conditioned by this technique itself. It is even possible that he would have been required to provide separations* for these drawings.

*Separations are made by the artist when he produces separate artwork (usually on transparent overlays) for the colour areas which are to be printed down on the black and white original drawings which he has provided.

85 Illustration from 'Stories of the Table Round', *Little Folks* 1902

Some of these pictures are published full page in *Little Folks*, about 20 cm by 15 cm (8 × 6 in; figure 85). In the book versions they are usually reduced to less than two thirds the size, so that the details as well as the quality of Rackham's line suffers accordingly: the colours are usually (an exception being the frontispiece to *The Land of Enchantment*) represented as an unpleasant half tone, or are removed completely. It could not have done Rackham's considerable reputation much good for the original designs of the *Little Folks* stories to appear thus mutilated under his name, especially in the manner of presentation adopted for *The Land of Enchantment*, in which a solid colour overlay is printed down over the line work. The general loss of quality may be observed by a comparison between the reduced illustration to *Stories of King Arthur* with the original size of the lovely two-colour original from *Little Folks*.

A delightful series of drawings for the *Little Folks* serial 'Littledom Castle' by M. H. Spielmann, were used in a collection entitled *Littledom Castle and Other Tales*, in 1903. Nine of the original eleven drawings were used in the book, none of which suffered in any way through this reappearance, and all of which are of a sufficient quality to hold their own with the other illustrations in the title, which are produced by some of the finest artists of the time. The delightful boredom of the ogre muttering 'Toujours soldat!' (figure 86) shows how well Rackham 'realized the mock seriousness and the burlesque fun of the tale— a tale which shows how ogres and dragons are shamelessly maligned'.*

86 'He murmured wearily, "Toujours soldat!"' *Little Folks* 1902

One other original *Little Folks* reprint unfortunately travesties the fine drawings which Rackham produced for the magazine: this was *The Rainbow Book* of 1909, the original contributions to which appeared in a 1905 serial entitled 'Adventures in Wizard Land', again by M. H. Spielmann. These rank

* From the Introduction to *Littledom Castle*.

87 'Its head was patted graciously', *Little Folks* 1905

among the most interesting and imaginative illustrations which Rackham did
specifically for children': the fantasy is exquisite, the line both delicate and
varied, the texture consummate, whilst the handling of rhythms within each
design was never surpassed by Rackham in ordinary line work. The two examples
at plates 26 and 87 show the artist—still fresh and innocent—handling with a
new eye all those elements which in later times he adopted (sometimes with less
love) as a set of formulas for his Rackhameries. Rackham chose to construct the
frontispiece for this book from one of the original vignette drawings, and whilst
this original is excellent in quality, by the time it has been reduced, placed in a
frame, and coloured, much of its spontaneity, quality of line and feeling for
space has been lost. The soft tones of pinks, ochres and yellows used by Rackham
are altogether at variance with the original illustrations, even though these are
indeed the colours which might well be used of a scene beneath the waters.

88 'Its head was patted graciously', *The Rainbow Book* 1909

This comparison is a fine example of how Rackham's original drawings are frequently lost when they are coloured, transplanted from their original setting, or imprisoned in a frame.

The anthology of children's stories collected in *Queen Mab's Fairy Realm* of 1901 are a delight on all scores, but the five drawings contributed by Rackham for May Bowley's stories 'The Princess who Understood Magic' and 'The Claws of the Peccalouchi' are certainly not among the best in the collection. Among the artists worth mentioning are Savage and Millar, the former of whom provided the delightful titlepage and frontispiece, the latter of whom gave us the excellent drawings for 'The Giant Knarratschki' and the images for 'The Sun Princess', which have a delicate feeling for space and texture.

The previous observations concerning Rackham's reprint books, and the survey of his excellent line illustrations for magazine, indicate how misfounded is the popular conception which holds that Rackham 'begins in 1905 with *Rip van Winkle*'. As the bibliography at page 170 makes clear, prior to the publication of this important book, Rackham had provided illustrations for well over fifty titles, and had gained a considerable reputation as an illustrator with a fine feeling for fantasy. However, it is with *Rip van Winkle* and not with *A Midsummer Night's Dream* of 1908, as one historian* has claimed, that Rackham blossomed into fame. We have already noted the quality of the plates in this remarkable book (see pages 87 and 93) though it is worth observing that there is a feeling for unity running throughout the whole series of pictures, a unity which is only too frequently absent in some of his other big picture-books.

*Martin Hardie in *Water-Colour Painting in Britain*. Since this book is frequently consulted by art students I have included a separate Appendix apropos of the errors concerning the entry under Arthur Rackham in this book. See Appendix D.

89 'Rip's daughter and grandchild', *Rip van Winkle* 1905

This delicate unity was preserved in the next book, however, which was also its equal in depth of fantasy and vision, thus serving to confirm the beginning of a decade which was to be the most important period of Rackham's life so far as the production of his illustrated books is concerned. This book was J. M. Barrie's *Peter Pan in Kensington Gardens*, which appeared in 1906. Two of the most outstanding colour plates in this volume are subtle combinations of

90 'The Kensington Gardens are in London, where the King lives', *Peter Pan in Kensington Gardens* 1906

91 'Put his strange case before old Solomon Caw', *Peter Pan in Kensington Gardens* 1906

portrait from real life, merging in a convincing world of fairy land. In the frontispiece, there is a picture of King Edward (figure 90) standing outside the Garden railings almost as though he were in a zoo with all the other humans, being examined by the pixies, gnomes, animals and birds. A self-portrait of Rackham is convincingly presented in the guise of a gnome, peering over the tulips within the Garden (figure 38). The elements of humanity are to a certain extent merged into this strange devic* world of Kensington Garden, in which nestles the Serpentine, a stretch of water which is there purely to protect Peter's island, 'but this is a very quiet secret place. It is where the birds are born who afterwards become baby boys and girls . . .' As on the earth itself, the devic forms, the animals, birds and humans hold a contiguous evolutionary ascent and descent, although within this imagery, as within the story, there is more emphasis given to the devic than to the human. This is the reason why the King seems so out of place, almost like a zoological specimen, and why it is the child, rather than Old Solomon Caw, or the improbable pair of shoe-cleaning mice at the foot of the gnarled tree (figure 91) who gives the impression of being an intruder. This sense of intrusion or of isolation is cleverly imposed by Rackham: the King is placed behind bars, and here the child is put on a branch of a tree, and is thus attempting to insert himself into the device world, in order to find contact with it.

Undoubtedly, the finest plate in *Peter Pan* is that which depicts Solomon Caw examining the five-pound note (figure 45), with two mice which might have come straight from a Disney studio, had they not been of an earlier age.†
In this clever plate the human element, which as we have seen is virtually excluded from the devic Gardens, is neatly reduced to a piece of paper—perhaps a symbol of the very end to which certain strains in the human world tend—and it is hardly surprising that the devic beings should be astonished and puzzled by it.

*Peter Pan* was the second of Rackham's books to be published in a trade and de luxe edition; with *Rip van Winkle* the venture had been something of a gamble, with *Peter Pan* it was a certainty. Its publication and quality was a sure sign that Rackham had arrived, and was now to remain as one of the leading illustrators in a wide field of book titles.

* *Devic*. An adjective derived from the Sanscrit *Deva*, from the root *div* (which also gave us 'devil' as well as 'divinity'). The term is applied to a wide range of invisible celestial entities which dwell on the planes above those proper to man. The evolution of the devas is centred on the earth, but their forms are generally invisible to ordinary sight. I have chosen this word which was popularized by the Theosophists towards the end of the last century, because it carries connotations which more accurately denote the world of Peter Pan, and indeed the world of Rackham, than the imprecise traditional European terms, such as 'fairy' or 'astral', which are now merely emotive or misunderstood. See G. Hodson's *Fairies at Work and at Play,* 1925.
†For many years I seriously believed that these two must be the prototypes of Gus and Jak in Disney's *Cinderella*, and even had lecture slides to prove it. Recently however I discussed this theory with my ten-year-old daughter who disagreed vehemently pointing out that Rackham's drawings 'look like mice except that one is wearing spectacles, and in any case Gus was fat and Jak was thin'. Then after a moment's serious thought she exploded much art theory with the conclusion, 'In any case you can't compare them.'

92 Vignette from chapter heading in *Rip van Winkle* 1905

93 'A company of odd-looking persons playing at ninepins', *Rip van Winkle* 1905

113

# RACKHAM'S BEST BOOK
## ILLUSTRATIONS 2
### From the new *Alice* to the new *Toad*

THE de luxe era was upon Rackham, and its immediate effect was that of making his life easier from the economic point of view: after 1906 he was no longer worried about money or status, and by 1920 he was comparatively rich. Not only were the royalties on his books satisfactory and fairly constant, but he had established the practice of selling the artwork originals, from which reproductions had been made, mainly through the Leicester Galleries in London.

One of the long-term effects of the de luxe market was that his books took on a rarified feeling, a special quality of style, which required that he continue to produce work with a pronounced Rackhamerie about it. The market demanded henceforth that he should retain in his pictures the quality and outlook which he had so convincingly and successfully announced to the world through *Rip van Winkle* and *Peter Pan*, with deviations from these only sufficient to meet the exigencies of fidelity to the text and author. In effect, however, this meant that Rackham had entered that Shamballa of which all freelance illustrators dream, and few believe exists: he was able to dictate to publishers which books he would illustrate, and which he would not. It can be no accident that after 1906, save for reprints of previous works, and the odd commission he executed for friends, the titles he worked on were generally suited to his peculiar pen which had that distinctive facility for invoking the devas, fairies and inhabitants of an archaic, wholly imaginary, or even epic world.

In 1907 he established further proof of his distinctive vision with his fascinating series of pictures for *Alice in Wonderland*. Other artists had strayed willingly or unwillingly into this Tenniel territory, but the general unrest and the factions which were created by Rackham's series of drawings for this text was a sure sign that the artist was by now among the most famous illustrators of the time. In one corner growled those who regarded this invasion of Tenniel as unfair, or even doomed to failure: these individuals did not wish to have their graphic prejudices disturbed. In the other corner smiled the supporters of Rackham, one of whom (presumably unaware of the different printing methods, and of the heavy strictures under which Tenniel worked), wrote to Rackham saying that his 'delightful Alice is alive and makes by contrast Tenniel's Alice look a stiff wooden puppet'. The arguments for and against the 'new' *Alice* are now merely so much clash of old steel, for whilst Tenniel quite rightly persists in many editions to this day, Rackham's pictures have also become part of our cultural heritage, and we are the richer for both. Whilst there may be no doubt that artists of the future will give us their version of this classic, it would be a brave and talented illustrator who would dare to emulate Rackham in the courageous way that Rackham emulated Tenniel (see figure 95).

The truth is that Rackham's pen and brush, with the aid of his youthful model Miss Dommett, created a feeling for *Alice* which carries way beyond anything that Tenniel conceived, and it is worth observing that the emphasis of this *Alice* is quite different from that he gave to *Peter Pan*. In Barrie's fantasy the curious world of humans was viewed (when it was viewed at all) from the standpoint of the various devic creatures, and through the eyes of the animals and birds—the King was excluded from the Gardens, and the old gentleman who walked through the park surrounded by sylphs and fairies was clearly out of his depths in that context. This was not so in *Alice*, for all the animal curiosities (figure 46), and the many anthropomorphized forms, were always subjugated to Alice, and we never forget that we are seeing this strange world through the perplexed eyes of a young human being. Alice is herself at no time an 'invader' from another realm, but clearly a person who is experiencing that world through a dream.

Although the distinction between the devic world of *Peter Pan* and the dream world of *Alice* is a subtle one, it may be summarized by saying that the creatures of Alice's dream are presented as caricatures, with that peculiar intensity which is experienced in the dream world. The Mad Hatter and the White Rabbit belong more nearly to the world of the cartoon than to the world of the devas or faerie, so that Alice is able to maintain her identity even when completely immersed in this curious world. In his rendering of the mad tea party (figure 95), Rackham supports Alice as the focal point of attention, from which all visual judgements must stem, by having her face at the converging point of a series of compositional line pointers: the edges of the long table, the folds of the table-cloth, the lines of the window ledge and bars, the lines of the thatching, as well as the trunks of the tree, all lead to Alice's face, as she sits framed in the massive chair of state.

It is another outward sign of Rackham's genius that he was able to create within the different titles of his books several stratifications of the devic world, as required by the concepts, philosophies and themes of his various authors: the devic sphere of the Niblung is entirely different from the devic sphere of the Kensington Garden hierarchy—the first is clearly of a descending order of being, whilst the second is ascending. What is frequently overlooked by those who condemn Rackham as merely an illustrator of fairybooks is that he deals not with one single world of faerie, but with several streams of devic ascent and descent.

*The Ingoldsby Legends*, of 1907, for which Rackham refurbished, coloured and partly reworked many of the drawings originally in the 1898 edition of the same work, makes a fascinating comparison with the two previous books,

94 'A curtain-lecture is worth all the sermons in the world for teaching
the virtues of patience and long-suffering', *Rip van Winkle* 1905

95 'A Mad Tea Party', *Alice's Adventures in Wonderland* 1907

96 'Kill me a red-hipped bumble-bee on the top of a
thistle', *A Midsummer Night's Dream* 1908

*Peter Pan* and *Alice*, for they show how much Rackham has advanced in style,
feeling for subject, and visualization in only nine years. In comparison to the
later books, these plates, for all their excellent qualities, are stilted and un-
convincing, even dated, and it is only in the completely new plates (figure 22)
that we see the new fluent Rackham, though even in these he has found it
necessary to tone down his vision in order to establish a unity within the series
of drawings. In this particular plate we see Rackham dealing convincingly with
an old problem which faces all illustrators at one time or another, that of convey-
ing the sense of movement on a flat surface, without recourse to the crude
graphic devices which are acceptable in comics and certain magazines.

The composition brilliantly suggests the upward sweep, in a double spiral
*S* shape which would have done justice to Blake himself. The bottom of this
double *S* starts in the wind-swept trees to the bottom left, and runs up the
two legs of the man in the foreground, and then curves around his body, into
the cloak of the witch, out across the gap between the end of her broom, and her
steeple hat, into the hazel twigs and legs of the witch above, and then terminates

in the two bodies of the highest witches, these two curves running together in the dramatic point of the cat familiar, which appears to be flying against its will. The hair of the witches, the bent hazel-twigs of their brooms, all sway to this upward movement, and thus suggest the eddies of air which would accompany the sweep of the transvection: but it is in the delicate lines which trace backwards from the four paws of the unfortunate cat which resort to the comic device of linear 'force marks' or 'drawn air eddies' to suggest movement. This is one of the rare occasions when Rackham uses such obvious linear conventions in his colour plates; later on in the *Ring* series (figure 98, for example) when he seeks to suggest the movement of the Rhinemaidens, he does this through the use of hair rhythms, or through the eddies of water, for he would have realized from this example in Ingoldsby that the use of lines which have no other primary justification merely brings the drawing to the level of near-cartoon.

During the two years after the successes of *Alice*, Rackham had a wide choice of potential titles to choose from: publishers were aware that anything he touched with his pen would turn to gold almost overnight. Even so, or perhaps because of this, they played safe by having him illustrate some classics. Within twelve months appeared Shakespeare's *A Midsummer-Night's Dream*, De la Motte Fouqué's *Undine*, and the Grimm brothers' *Fairy Tales*, all very different in quality and feeling, as demanded by the texts, but all of extremely high quality.

97 'I am that merry wanderer of the night',
*A Midsummer Night's Dream* 1908

98 'The Rhine-Maidens obtain possession of the ring and bear it off in triumph',
*The Rhinegold and The Valkyrie* 1910

99 'The water Nymphs, That in the bottom plaid,
Held up their pearled writs and took her in', *Comus* 1921

A MIDSUMMER-
NIGHT'S
DREAM.

ACT I.
SCENE I.

*Athens.   The palace of* THESEUS.

*Enter* THESEUS, HIPPOLYTA, PHILOSTRATE,
*and* Attendants.

THESEUS.

Now, fair Hippolyta, our nuptial hour
Draws on apace ; four happy days bring in
Another moon : but, O, methinks, how slow
This old moon wanes ! she lingers my desires,
Like to a step-dame or a dowager
Long withering out a young man's revenue.

100  First page, *A Midsummer Night's Dream* 1908

The *Dream* was, of course, an almost perfect setting for Rackham's devic imagination—perhaps only bettered by the opportunity of *The Tempest*—with the result that some of the fairies, elves and goblins he created for this play are among his finest colour images (figure 103), and almost all the plates echo perfectly the mysterious interweaving of lightness and depth in this great work. Many of the formal plates are exquisite, whether they depict the principal events of the main theme of the story, such as the translated Bottom with his ass-head (figure 104) mocked by tree sprites, or the night-rule of Titania's haunted grove,

101 Vignette from *A Midsummer Night's Dream* 1908

I do wander every where,
Swifter than the moon's sphere ;

those incidents within the subsidiary action, with details hardly dreamed of by Shakespeare, such as the gnomish knife-grinder in a motley group of fairies. Some of the floriated headings for the *Dream* are the finest of Rackham's line at the time, as for example the heading vignette for Act One, Scene One, which with typical Rackham irrelevance spreads its tendrils over the page, and into the text (figure 100), ignoring the fact that the setting is supposed, according to Shakespeare, to be the palace of Theseus, and throwing us immediately into a tangle-wood Rackhamerie, with mice, pixies and a sleeping maiden.

With the aqueous world of *Undine* Rackham found an opportunity to revive and develop his earlier *art nouveau* linear decorative drawing, especially in the need to incorporate waves and water currents in his pictures. He was thus able to connect a felicitious quality of decoration into his plates, as well as a new feeling for flat pattern which harks back to *fin de siècle* without being too openly mannered. In some respects, however, the treatment of the waves around Undine in figure 102 goes a little too far, and the grotesque faces insinuated into the waters are only crudely incorporated into the linear rhythms, and belong neither to the style of Undine, nor to the style of the waves. Within this plate,

102 'Soon she was lost to sight in the Danube', *Undine* 1909

103 'One aloof stand sentinel', *A Midsummer Night's Dream* 1908

104 'I will sing, that they shall hear I am not afraid', *A Midsummer Night's Dream* 1908

therefore, we find four unintegrated styles: the drawing of Undine herself, the linear rhythm of the waves, the grotesque faces within the waves, and the landscape in the top third of the composition. Our sensibilities cannot assimilate this lack of stylistic integration, and the plate remains a failure. Such criticism is worth pointing out only to indicate the high quality of Rackham's handling when he does succeed in pulling together different stylistic strains within one single drawing through the use of linear rhythms. In figure 105, from the same text, the compositional device in itself pulls together the different elements within the waters. The strong upward curve of the shoal of fish sets the theme of a strong single undulating curve; this is then taken up by the curve of the

105  'The infancy of Undine', *Undine* 1909

106  Illustration from 'The Seven Ravens', *Fairy Tales* of Grimm, 1909

floating drapery which swells upwards from the left arm of Undine. These two curves cross in approximately the centre of the picture, leaving the child within the bottom area isolated, yet caught in the curved line of rocks and pebbles which sweep behind it. The curves of the shell and of the patterns of the flowing dress, help to pull this figure into the harmony of the composition.

The robustness of Grimm's *Fairy Tales* invited quite a different treatment, both in quality of line and in compositional structure, yet in these plates for the 1909 edition, there is the same sense of restriction and archaic treatment which we observed in the reworking of Ingoldsby from the 1898 version, for some of these plates from Grimm are refurbished drawings of the 1900 edition.

Few of us will have experienced the intense mystical joy with which C. S. Lewis saw his first Rackham illustration for *Siegfried and the Twilight of the Gods*: 'His pictures, which seemed to me then to be the very music made visible, plunged me a few fathoms deeper into my delight. I have seldom coveted anything as I coveted that book: and when I heard that there was a cheaper edition at fifteen shillings (though the sum was to me almost mythological) I knew I could never rest till it was mine. I got it in the end, largely because my brother went shares with me, purely through kindness, as I now see and then more than half suspected, for he was not enslaved by the Northernness.'* Lewis's rhapsody, though it is distinctly personal, and an integral part of his own voyage of the soul, reminds us of something about the nature of art which is all too frequently

*C. S. Lewis *Surprised by Joy*. I should have liked to reproduce in full the relevant three pages from this autobiography, as they are so relevant to my own theme, and because they open up speculations on the inner realm of what Lewis calls 'Northernness', but space prevents it.

127

107 'Old Mother Goose', *Mother Goose* 1913

128

lost to those who write art histories and make judgements on artwork of the past—that powerful influence of what George Bernard Shaw called 'contemporaneous success', which is related to the fact that art is produced not for the future which assesses it, but for the present which requires it as pabulum for the soul. Within the present context, a few words from Lewis throw much light on Rackham's success in terms of the influence he exercised during the first decade of our century, for he speaks of his own soul-need of the time, and in so doing reflects on the soul-need of many many people at that time: 'First, you will misunderstand everything unless you realize that, at the time, Asgard and the Valkyries seemed to me incomparably more important than anything else in my experience—than the Matron Miss C., or the dancing mistress, or my chances of scholarship. More shockingly, they seemed much more important than my steadily growing doubts about Christianity. They may have been—in part, no doubt, was—penal blindness; yet that might not be the whole story. If the Northernness seemed a bigger thing than my religion, that may partly have been because my attitude towards it contained elements which my religion ought to have contained and did not.'

The text of the *Ring* series, published in 1910 and 1911, naturally turned Rackham away from any sweetness and light that fairy tale might shed in love sought in forest and river, and such a dark gothic world of fact and fancy, with

108 'Magical rape
    Pierces my heart;
    Fixed is my gaze,
    Burning with terror;
    I reel, my heart faints and fails!',
    *Siegfried and The Twilight of the Gods* 1911

its dark nordic forests, gnarled earth beings, fire-breathing dragons, and delicate water spirits, so immersed Rackham in his own telluric element that he lost sight of Siegfried the Sun god. The neo-gothic Rackham knew only too well how to handle the bad devic elements of Mime and Alberich, but his drawings of Siegfried, man or child (figures 108 and 109) are apologetic and awkward, especially when he sets out specifically to present them in a romantic vein. Golden-haired Siegfried, with the sun behind him, or with nimbus rays proceeding from his own self, is obviously a deified sun, standing before the sleeping Brunnhilde, but in face he is totally unheroic, perhaps a grown-up Lord Fauntleroy in golden wig (figure 108). Rackham could not handle the heroic and epic, and this fact reduces the quality of many of the drawings within this series. However, in high relief from the gloom of Alberich's caves we have a series of plates of the Rhinemaidens, which alone make the series worthwhile.

In these plates, especially in the final picture of *Siegfried* (figure 98) which shows the maidens obtaining possession of the ring, and bearing it off in triumph, there is a lyric beauty of colour, line and form which Rackham rarely achieves again. The whole plate is suffused with a subtle transformation of forms—spray becomes foam, foam becomes jewellery and clothing, clothing becomes hair, and in turn hair transforms itself into diaphanous waves which are those of water currents and air eddies. This lovely metamorphosis of foam, waves, bodies and hair insists itself as a graphic wedge between the two unlike elements of air and water, which are in turn rendered alike by the transforming pen. The upper

109 'Mime and the infant Siegfried',
*Siegfried and The Twilight of the Gods* 1911

110 'Wee Folk' from *Arthur Rackham's Book of Pictures* 1913

region is of air, but it is wave-like and aqueous in quality, whilst the lower region of water is almost ariel in its swelling undulation. This is Rackham's personal style taken to its highest point of expressive delicacy.

So far as titles go (but certainly not so far as artwork goes) we move into a different key with *Mother Goose*, a book constructed in 1913 from a series of plates and line drawings which had appeared and would appear in *St Nicholas* between 1912 and 1914.* The poems were chosen by Rackham, presumably in terms of the themes and subjects he wished to illustrate: this would account for the consistently good quality of the many plates and of the numerous line drawings. Among the most noticeable of pictures in this book are 'Hark! Hark! the dogs do bark!' which has Rackham delighting in rags and tatters a deal more colourful than might be expected in our own age, and the altogether curious colour plate 'Old Mother Goose', remarkable for its composition, in which the black forests and borders merge to form an underlying pictorial structure reminiscent of Nolde or Munch, the colour also being virtually expressionist in

*Appendix B on page 183 sets out the list of St Nicholas illustrations which were used in the 1913 *Mother Goose* and in *Arthur Rackham's Picture Book*.

feeling. This plate (figure 107) is an aberration, so far as the rest of the book is concerned, for within this we have the usual Rackham motley of lovely women, Rackham-faced gnomes, and all the images we might expect of the title. Quite appropriately, Rackham illustrates 'As I was going to St Ives' with his own portrait, in a situation which is almost akin to a schizophrenic's dream, with the dance of seven witches, and the multiples of seven cats and kittens (figure 3).

*Arthur Rackham's Picture Book*, also of 1913, has been vastly over-rated. The book consists of a series of forty-four coloured plates and a few line drawings, with an amusing introduction by Sir Arthur Quiller-Couch. It represents an attempt by Rackham and his publishers to trade upon his name, unfortunately to the detriment of that name, since not all the plates included in the book are from good artwork, or are representative of Rackham at his best. The majority of the plates are simply refurbished or coloured-up versions of black and white illustrations which had appeared in books and titles over a period of about fifteen years. In his Introduction Sir Arthur waxes poetic about the collection, speaking of it as a kind of 'biography', but it seems that Sir Arthur was not

111 'Hi! You up there', *Arthur Rackham's Book of Pictures* 1913

112 'Borne by the Winds and Currents', 'The Song of Perseus',
*The Greek Heroes* 1903

aware of the extent of the refurbishing, or of the extent to which the selection
was something of a pot-boiler of hastily selected, previously used works, since
he lists a few which had appeared before, clearly believing these to be exceptions.
The fact that the book is a pot-boiler accounts for the presence in one book of
such a disturbing range of different and indifferent techniques and styles which
find a unity, if at all, only from the heavy khaki card upon which each of the
plates is mounted. The total effect is not so much stimulating (a properly
conceived collection might well have been), as disturbing, for jumbled together
are the delicate line and colour wash drawing such as 'On the Beach' (figure 127),
with the heavy coloured illustration to 'Jack the Giant Killer' (figure 111), and
the very insignificant Langham sketches* which round off the book.

Connoisseurs of Rackham will find many old favourites here, though not
always in their accustomed guise, and certainly not always shown to advantage.
The 'Danae' is a coloured version of the charming original line illustration to
'The Story of Perseus' in *The Greek Heroes* of 1903 (figure 112): the colour
improves the drawing only slightly, whilst the whole design suffers enormously
from the cropping of its lower edge. Plate 11 is from this same original book, 'The
Dragon of the Hesperides', though in this case it is improved by the addition of
colour, for the muted blues, greens and greys send the yellow apples into a
vibrant magic which makes the plate work well. The sea-serpent of plate 25 is our
old friend from *Little Folks* (figure 42), which was used also in *The Rainbow Book*
of 1909, originally a delightful rhythmic line drawing in Rackham's so-called
*art nouveau* style, now rather heavy and sad with colour, obviously unhappy in
his chains of frame. The 'Wizard' of plate 26 is also derived from the same 1905
serial 'Adventures in Wizard Land' as the sea-serpent, though here the wizard

*See page 50 above for some account of the Langham sketches and of these last plates of the
*Picture Book*.

113  Illustration from *Queen Mary's Gift Book* 1919

is nicely edged into his containing frame with a structure of goblins and very Rackham toucans, in a compositional device we have studied before. *The Gossips* of plate 30 is a poorly coloured version of what was originally an exciting pencil drawing which promised well as a final ink and colour picture, and which had been reproduced in *Little Folks* in October 1907; according to Quiller-Couch this drawing started life as a Langham sketch. At least ten of the plates were used in *St Nicholas* in the following year, and must surely have been commissioned for that magazine before appearing in the *Picture Book*. However, it would be tedious to list the provenance of all the pictures: almost all the good ones may be traced to earlier usage, or to uncoloured prototypes, whilst the poor ones (of which there are several) are best forgotten. The selection of plates was not made with any aim to represent Rackham at his best, or even to represent Rackham at all—they were selected from pictures which were to hand, or which could be refurbished quickly—a selection made purely on the basis of convenience. It is instant Rackham, and like most instant things, not good.

During the years of the First World War the illustration market naturally fell off considerably, but Rackham was among those artists sufficiently well established to join the chorus of literary and artistic outcries in the traditional manner against the darker aspects of the war. Few of the plates and drawings he contributed to the various Gift Books*, or to *The Allies Fairy Book* of 1916 are worth serious consideration, with the exception of the magnificently composed ornithologist's nightmare (figure 128) which is the best plate of this war book.

*See the bibliography in Appendix A for the years 1914–15.

However, this period was not quite a doldrums for Rackham, for it was during these years that he illustrated a new Brothers Grimm title, *Little Brother and Little Sister* which is in effect one of his crowning achievements. In these thirteen colour plates we find the most astonishing versatility of style, and an exquisite pitch of execution. The style ranges from the delicate to the virtual burlesque caricature. On the one hand is an example of pre-Raphaelite, infinitely tender portrayals of womanhood, such as 'The True Sweetheart' (figure 114), or the

114 'The third time she wore the star-dress which sparkled at every step', 'The True Sweetheart', *Little Brother and Little Sister* 1917

115 'The waiting maid sprang down first and Maid
Maleen followed', 'Maid Maleen' *Little Brother and
Little Sister* 1917

delicate realism of Maid Maleen and her waiting woman escaping from the
terrible tower of her father (figure 115). Yet within the same book we find the
classic Rackhamerie of the gnome with his beard caught in the cleft of the
semi-anthropomorphized tree, appealing to Rose-red and Snow-white for help
(figure 116) and the Hassell-like custard-pie of the three soldiers and the long

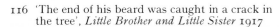

116 'The end of his beard was caught in a crack in
the tree', *Little Brother and Little Sister* 1917

nose (figure 117). This is one of the few books illustrated by Rackham from which it would be possible to select any single colour picture in order to demonstrate Rackham's art at its finest.

It was inevitable that during this jingoistic and patriotic era the title chosen by or for Rackham should have harked back to epic tales of English valour, or to the innocence of childhood: Malory and his *Romance of King Arthur*, Flora Annie Steel's *English Fairy Tales*, Swinburne's poems of childhood, *The Springtide of Life*, and the collection *Some British Ballads*. In these titles we certainly

117 'They came at last to their poor old friend', 'The Nose Tree',
*Little Brother and Little Sister* 1917

find some excellent Rackham's but nothing extraordinary. These, however, were punctuated after the end of the War with the series of silhouette illustrations which Rackham provided for *Cinderella* in 1919 and for *The Sleeping Beauty* in 1920. There is a renewed confidence, a delicacy of vision, in these pictures which is surprising and refreshing for those familiar with the sophisticated colour plates for which Rackham was famed at the time. Not, of course, that Rackham was in any sense new to the use of silhouettes, but these books are the first from his pen to depend entirely upon this interesting and difficult technique. His simple forms are often inventive, imaginative, amusing, and tell their stories well. But it is in the more sophisticated silhouettes, in which he combines texture and reversals, as in the illustration of the naked queen and the frog (figure 118) in which the variety of leaf texture and the reverse silhouette of the urns, ballustrade and statue has been used with exquisite skill, and yet remains as a background to place the two figures in a romantic setting, that Rackham's ingenuity is fully expressed. Perhaps the only jarring feature in the entire image is the large sponge, which is pleasant enough in texture, but unpleasant in shape. The three double-page spread colour silhouettes, which Rackham probably prepared as separations, do not work very well. The whole essence of silhouette illustration lies in the strength of the single impact and contrast of black and white, and the effect of introducing two extra colours (though these may be silhouettes themselves) tends to destroy the simplicity and unity of the whole.

118 Silhouette of the naked queen and the frog from *Sleeping Beauty*, 1920

119 'Will he desert his summer throne', *A Dish of Apples* 1921

There is a gentle, almost imperceptible, softening of style in Rackham's working during the early twenties. Rackham is mellowing, his love for the fantastic giving place to a love for what we so readily call 'the real'. We see this in the colour plates for *Comus*, in *A Dish of Apples*, both of 1921, and especially in Hawthorne's *A Wonder Book* of the following year. The softening is noticeable in the manner in which he paints his children and women: the daughters of Hesperus, the Fair Ligea and the nymphs of *Comus*; the three children picking windfalls in *A Dish of Apples* (figure 119), and in the plates of Pandora in Hawthorne (figure 130). The technical softening is a result of Rackham's tendency more and more to lose his defining outline in the washwork of colour; the lines still persist, but the pictures are tending to be less coloured drawings, and are gradually becoming more and more like paintings. The spiritual softening is due to what is happening to Rackham the man. He is by now a little past his peak of development, yet he now has the total respect of the world: he is a capable,

139

confident and mellowed master of his chosen idiom. A wistful realism is becoming more and more noticeable in his work, and is insinuating itself into the flow of his forms: there is less emphasis on the insistent curvilinear rhythms in his plates, and within these form begins to grow rotund at the expense of line. In many cases this adds a new meaning and poignancy.

When in the December 1922 issue of *The Bookman* G. S. Layard mildly remonstrated with Rackham on the grounds that he liked him 'best when he gets away from the formulas he has invented and to which he constantly recurs', he might well have had in mind the *Comus* of 1921. Rackham's vision was not suited to Milton's allegorizing play, and he has recourse to many formulas to sustain the interest of the reader. Pale and very English, rather than bronzed and Greek, nymphs inhabit the cold nordic seas, reminiscent of a re-hash of certain images more appropriate to the *Ring* cycle, whilst three colour plates in sequence have distinctly anthropomorphized trees in a world very Rackham, but not very Milton, and these, with the usual accretion of witches, demons, beasties and gnomes set fair to show merely that 'no evil thing' has 'hurtfull power o'er true virginity'—an example of over-illustration, if ever there was one. Among the coloured plates of animal-men, grotesque trees and lovely nymphs parading Rackham, we find scattered the occasional gem of a vignette, as for example figure 120, 'Sabrina descends', but on the whole few of these make the superficial treatment of Milton worthwhile.

Rackham's trees, somewhat out of place in *Comus*, come into their own in *A Dish of Apples*, for all the main illustrations and the three colour plates contain trees. These range from anthropomorphized Rackhamesque to twisted, almost Chinese-style apple trees (figure 119), curiously without leaves, but very fruitful; to fairy-land trees sporting apples with leaves, and a fine crop of gnomes, fairies or pixies (figure 121). One of the trees is a home for pixies, and is thoughtful

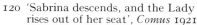

120 'Sabrina descends, and the Lady rises out of her seat', *Comus* 1921

121 'Lady's apple thou shalt be', *A Dish of Apples* 1921

enough to have grown a hand that the toucan-Rackham bird may perch on its index finger.

The moment one opens Hawthorne's *Wonder Book* one becomes aware of the rounding and softening of form in Rackham's work. The modern Pandora of Hawthorne opens her box for the world in 1921, and she is a very living young girl (figure 130), with breasts just beginning to swell, indicating that Rackham was aware of the undertones of this story which is being retold with every lifetime. In 'The Paradise of Children' from the same text the children are drawn in line, but the washes of colour give them a rotundity of form and a very human life. The point which Rackham is making, surely, is that these are real children, a real Pandora, and not some dream from fairy land. Midas is not real, almost a

caricature, as one given to gold must be. Yet we feel the shock of his becoming a living father when he loses his daughter to gold (figure 122), his caricature face now hidden in the theatrical gesture—the only dramatic picture in this gentle book, in spite of the fight, which is bathos, put up by the chimera against Bellerophon.

For once it is not to the mounted full-colour plates that we immediately turn our attention in this book, but to the fascinating series of illustrations printed in three muted colours, and probably prepared by Rackham as separations. Rackham must have looked closely at the lithographs of Vuillard and Bonnard before he produced these prints, and again at the Japanese prints which were the common heritage of all three artists. Whilst not all of the three-

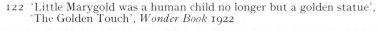

122 'Little Marygold was a human child no longer but a golden statue',
'The Golden Touch', *Wonder Book* 1922

123 'A man who did not like dogs. In fact he hated them, when he saw
one he used to go black in the face, and he threw rocks at it until
it got out of sight', 'The Birth of Bran', *Irish Fairy Tales* 1920

colour prints are good in design, they do point to a new illustrative approach
which Rackham unfortunately did not see fit to pursue. The finest of these
show the decorative Rackham at his best (figure 134) combining within the soft
decorative elements the Rackhamesque lines in a delicacy of style which is the
logical conclusion to the three-coloured silhouettes of *Cinderella* and *Sleeping
Beauty* of the previous year. Now the harshness of the black flat pattern (and the
compulsion of its stark imagery) is gone; the colour does not stand out in
meaningless isolation but is integrated into one single harmony of muted tones.

Rackham's two great books of the twenties were James Stephens' *Irish
Fairy Tales* of 1920, and Shakespeare's *Tempest* of 1926, both of which exhibit
the general softening of style, as well as the results of an obvious urge within
Rackham to discover new forms of expression.

Beyond the softness of style and inventiveness, the most striking thing
about the colour plates for *Irish Fairy Tales* is the felicitous and appropriate use
of celtic borders. Certain of these plates exhibit a wide variety of different
borders, ranging from the simple strip-border of 'The man who did not like dogs'
(figure 123) to the fully integrated interlace borders of the illustration showing the
'wild and shy and monstrous creatures' which roamed in the forests at the
beginning of Ireland (figure 124). In this latter plate the red and pink interlace
scroll border at the top infolds itself as it descends to the right, to become part
of the birds, then of the trees, and finally link with the stag-horned monster,

143

124 'Wild and shy and monstrous creatures roam in her plains and forests',
'The Story of Tuan MacCahill', *Irish Fairy Tales* 1920

125 'My life became a ceaseless scurry and wound and escape,
a burden and anguish of watchfulness', 'The Story of Tuan MacCahill',
*Irish Fairy Tales* 1920

half hidden in the shrubbery below. The interfolding of scroll and birds is so clever that we are not sure whether the bird is carrying in its beak a red worm, or merely part of the scrollwork, and it is hard to determine whether the lower bird is perched on a tree, or on a floriated scroll band. In the bottom left the opposite transformation takes place, for the roots of the tree are transformed not into the expected bevy of gnomes or pixies, but into an interlace border. The metamorphosis and extrusion of tendril scrolls into branches, branches into animal horns, and tree roots back into tendrils is the very stuff of celtic art. In addition it is a most appropriate expression of the doctrine of the transmigration of souls, which is so thinly disguised in the story of Tuan Mac Carill, for which this picture is one of the illustrations.

In the plate which shows Tuan transformed into the King of Salmon, the softness of colours and forms is picked out by another exciting border, this time in black and white, perhaps offsetting the heaviness of Tuan, whose anguish is extreme (figure 125). At the foot we find a series of decorative fishes, partly integrated into celtic floriate borders, reminiscent of Anglo-Saxon, or of older art forms from a turbulent past, a style derived perhaps as far away as Northern China, with the horsemen of the Scyths and the Ordos. Above, and on the vertical band to the right, is a series of leaf and flower decorations which leap millenia, and bring us firmly back to the twenties to a group of motives which is exciting and fresh, yet at the same time, for all its late 'new style' modernism, is still appropriate to the theme. It is clever of Rackham to integrate the ancient and the modern in one border surround, for the story contained within it is both as old as man, and yet it is a story of modern times. The theme is the story of Everyman, and pictures a man driven world-weary in pursuit of some dream, threatened by hostile forces on all sides, so that his life becomes a 'ceaseless scurry and woe and escape, a burden and anguish of watchfulness'.

The border of plate 123, 'A man who did not like dogs', is simpler, but here again the aim of Rackham is not merely to decorate, but to further the action of the story. The function of the bottom border is to add an 'Irish' quality to the illustration. Rackham has the tails of the two canine monsters of the base richly floriate upon themselves and scroll off into cyphers more appropriate to a celtic manuscript; these creatures are separated from each other by an interlace roundel which might have been plucked from *The Book of Kells* itself. This celtic border of semi-interlace reminds us that this is not just any man, and any dog, but the Fergus Fionnliath of Galway, chasing a dog of Ireland.

Some of Rackham's illustrations for *The Tempest* of 1926 reveal very clearly a graphic problem implicit in many of Rackham's works. The problem arises from the fact that in many instances, especially in texts telling of ordinary people caught unexpectedly in the world of fairy land, or in a world otherwise alien to them, it is necessary for the artist to combine in the same picture elements which are of the ordinary world, and elements which are from the world of fantasy. We saw the problem to some extent in *Peter Pan* and in *Alice*, in which Rackham gave emphasis to the fantasy world in the former, to the

126  '"Mind your own business" said Murrum the cat', *Poor Cecco* 1925

human world in the latter. The need to combine the real and the imaginary in one single style gives rise to a strained relationship within the pictorial area. When this problem arises for Rackham, his tendency is to sacrifice the real world of objective reality to strengthen the fantasy—as for example when he pictures anthropomorphized trees in the place of real trees, or when he works in such a way as to present his animals as half-human, thus bringing them a shade nearer to the 'objective' human world.

The obvious dichotomy between real and imaginary, between say, the human and the faerie, is frequently expressed by Rackham in his tendency to adopt different styles of line, colour and technique for these two worlds. In his remarkable *Little Brother and Little Sister* he has presented the real world of womanhood, as for example in the drawing of the true sweetheart (figure 114), and within the same book, the different style and technique required of the caricature imaginary world of fairy land and burlesque (figure 117) which had been the best subjects of his *Rip van Winkle*. In *Little Brother* we find one line drawing which represents in a very clear manner the different approaches to the two worlds: this picture shows a tailor and a hunchback who have been bewitched by the little folk, and are now threatened by an old man with a knife. The real element—the two humans and the tree—are drawn in a strong and vigorous line, whilst the imaginary elements—the little folk and the old man—are drawn in a thin, almost vaporous line. As such a drawing reveals, Rackham is aware of

147

127 'On the Beach', plate 21, *Arthur Rackham's Book of Pictures* 1913

128 'The birds show the young man the white dove's nest', *The Allies' Book* 1916

how difficult it is to yoke together these disparate elements, especially when it is necessary to establish within the illustration that there is a struggle between these real and imaginary worlds. We see this time and again in many of Rackham's illustrations, in which he has recourse to the technique of incorporating two distinct styles within the same plate or drawing, sometimes successfully, sometimes not.\* It is significant that in the illustrations for *The Tempest*, which has itself this theme of the intermingling of the real and imaginary, are Rackham's most satisfying solutions to the problems set by the need to mingle these two different worlds.

Not every plate is of the highest order, but three plates, 'Come unto these yellow sands'; 'The isle is full of noises' (figure 131), and the fine 'Sometimes a thousand twangling instruments will hum about mine ears' (figure 129), reach near perfection, and in so doing point a new quality in Rackham's work, indicating that he was at this time looking for a new style. The harmony between the imaginary and the real is established for once not at the expense of the living beings, so much as at the expense of the background and natural forms: Rackham makes a distinct and highly satisfactory attempt to make both the background and the real elements of the picture as decorative as possible, and to emphasize in the human or supra-human participants within the illustration any natural decorative qualities. In this way the two forms are harmonized, and each picture attains a graphic integrity which is rare in plates concerned with the meeting of two worlds. It is for such reasons as these that the wings of the fairies in 'Come unto these yellow sands' are drawn and coloured in a similar linear formation to the background rocks, and that intermediate to these wings and rocks are the colours and forms of the water in the foreground. Every linear element is subordinated to establishing a graphic relationship between the animate and inanimate forms.

The almost magical decorative qualities of the second illustration (figure 131) establish a similar graphic relationship of forms: the rocks become almost leaf-like, the decorative foliage of the trees become almost rock-like, in a subtle and graceful transmutation. The heads of the spirits displace the flowers on this magical tree, and it is cunningly contrived that one may not say where trunk begins and spiritual body ends: This is soft, very delicate celtic interlacing of an exquisite kind.

Scarcely less decorative, but more consistent in its use of texture, is the third illustration (figure 129) which has solved the conflict between the real and imaginary by fusing them both in a mass of decorative foliage, vine-like creepers and spirits. There is a marked Persian-miniature influence in these plates, as in certain others within this book.

The quality of this kind of work, the innovations in regard to the decorative forms which he sought to inject into his illustrations, were clearly Rackham's

---

\* Lucy Atwell also adopted this solution to the same problem though with less subtlety, in her version of *Peter Pan and Wendy* of 1925. It is possible that she learned the technique from Rackham.

129 'Sometimes a thousand twangling instruments will hum about mine ears',
*The Tempest* 1926

answer to a crisis which he faced in regard to his work. The Rackham formulas, which were so fresh and exciting in his youthful days, were now not quite so filled with vigour. The problem was that his name was linked with a particular style, with a particular mode of vision, which meant that he found it difficult to move into another mode of vision, no matter how much his creativity demanded this. Like all artists, Rackham required his style continually to develop, and this meant that time and again he had to examine outworn or dubious clichés and imaginative quirks upon which his personalized style depended, and if they were found wanting to reject them without further thought. Rackham was aware as any other thoughtful artist that bad style is simply an out-worn style, which might have had a validity of its own in a different time. Unfortunately, there are distinct signs that the public, and presumably also the publishers who seek to satisfy this public, did not wish Rackham to change. The decorative style of the *Tempest* was one solution to this problem, for through it Rackham sought to

151

130 Illustration to 'Pandora's Box' from *The Wonder Book* 1922

131 'The Isle is full of noises', *The Tempest* 1926

132 'The Elfin Banquet' from *Fairy Tales of Hans Anderson* 1932

develop certain tendencies latent in the style which had brought him to the public's gaze.

Now well into his sixties, Rackham was in any case gradually moving away from the vitalized energetic gothic vision of the world, and an imaginative richness, one might even say a lyrical tone was entering his work. With the distinct mellowing and spiritualization of vision which comes with age, there was an urge to find an external mellowing of style. Yet it appears from some of the drawings and paintings of the early thirties that Rackham was aware of the public's reluctance to accept this change; they wanted the old Rackham, the one who would give them fairies, monsters, dragons, gnomes and living trees. Rackham could not throw himself into the world with quite the same readiness of earlier days, and there is a sense of frustration, even of boredom, in some of his works as a result. If we examine closely the numerous grotesque faces in 'The Banquet' illustration to 'The Elfin Hill' of *The Fairy Tales of Hans Andersen*, we find that they are all Rackham cyphers, with little individuality of their own (figure 132).

It is clear from the illustrations in this book, which appeared in 1932, that Rackham at this time needed an extra push, a foreign element in his work, to jog him out of the production of stereotypes and cyphers, in order that this style and vision might be refreshed. In his own note to the edition Rackham admits that he had made no attempt in the illustrations to look through Danish eyes. This may well have been a pity, for during this period (and indeed, throughout his life, for it appears to have been an integral part of his vision) when Rackham made the attempt to stretch his natural vision into another world, to open himself to a new stylistic approach, the results were usually exciting. We have already seen examples of this tendency in the celtic illustrations to *Irish Fairy Tales*, and if it is argued that Rackham's vision was in any case celtic, so that in these stories he simply met his perfect literary equivalent, then it may be pointed out that when Rackham opened himself to an oriental style, such as the Persian, for the *Tempest* series, the results were equally as good. The foreign styles stimulated him and in turn enabled him to make his drawings more stimulating. Rackham himself spoke of the pleasure of 'that encountering of familiar things in unfamiliar guise which later is one of the joys of foreign travel'.* The sentiment might well be applied not only to the stories of Andersen, but to the work of Rackham himself.

A fine example of the boredom to which Rackham was stylistically prey, is to be found in *The Arthur Rackham Fairy Book*, which should, if the title has any significance, present a great deal, but which is in fact highly disappointing. Save for two colour plates, we might echo the words of the 1922 critic who would claim to 'get more pleasure out of the charming end papers and the little black-and-white conceits and grotesques scattered about these pages' than out of the pretty coloured pictures.† The critic was in fact writing of the Hawthorne *Wonder Book*, which he at least describes as a 'fine and attractive volume', but the *Fairy Book* could hardly be described in such terms. Many of the black and white drawings have been produced unthinkingly, and with little poetic taste or imagination. Rackham's heart was not in this book at all, and with one or two exceptions he must have been uncomfortable with the various prop Rackham images which he had thrust upon himself. Perhaps this general embarrassment accounts for his missing the obvious piece of Rackhamerie in the colour picture which shows the meeting of the heroine's father, in 'Beauty and the Beast', with the grotesque beast in the palace gardens. In a previous time Rackham

*From Rackham's own introduction to Andersen's *Fairy Tales* 1932.
†G. S. Layard 'The Colour of Christmas: Thirteen Christmas Colour-Books and Their Artists', *The Bookman* December 1922.

133 'Enter Peaseblossom, Cobweb, Moth, and Mustardseed' from
*A Midsummer Night's Dream* 1939

¶ The hoary periwigs of dandelions

134 'The hoary periwigs of dandelions', *Wonder Book* 1922

135 'He heard a loud noise, and saw coming towards him a
beast, so frightful to look at that he was ready to faint
with fear', 'Beauty and the Beast', *Arthur Rackham's
Fairy Book* 1933

would have delighted in the meeting; he would have thrilled to present the
shaggy visage, hideous bloodshot eyes, lewd mouth, warts and all, with great
skill of imaginative pen. But instead Rackham has turned the back of the
monster upon us, and we see him clothed and capped, a monster only in name
(figure 135). This is not the Rackham we used to know, for he leaves it to the
reader, rather than to line and colour, to conjure this beast 'so frightful to look
at that he was ready to faint with fear'.

The only two really successful plates in the book are those in which Rackham
escapes from his previous conceits and formulas, and is swallowed by an
orientalizing influence. Both the 'New Lamps for Old' (figure 136) and 'Sinbad
carries the Old Man of the Sea on his shoulders' exhibit a delightful delicacy of
colour, the decorative lyrical sensibility, and the compositional quality of
oriental art forms. The plates are a waft of fresh air into a world which is becoming

altogether too heavy and gloomy; Rackham was reaching for a lighter touch, a more lyrical vision, yet he was being held back by his own past.

The sense of heaviness and gloom is found also in the very book in which it should be absent. In Walton's classic *The Compleat Angler*, of 1931, no fewer than six plates have landscape backgrounds, plates which should remind us of Rackham's very serious reputation as a landscape painter, with a fine vision of natural forms. Even here, however, there is a heaviness which we would not normally associate with the earlier Rackham: the landscape backgrounds are dreary in colour, the trees monotonously drawn, the skies invariably dark, even the rainbow which arcs over the dining fishermen in the sixth plate is lack-lustre, as though made of lead rather than light and rain-spray. The interior scenes, for all their Rackhamesque promise of eighteenth-century clothes and setting, with good ale and simple bucolic conversation, are heavy as though they have been drawn mechanically within the framework of well-worn formulas. These illustrations bear the same relationship to the early Rackham that the caught and stuffed pikes, eels, chubb and dace of the book bear to the original fish: the inert, brown-varnished forms do not disguise the fact that life has fled the body. It is perhaps significant that the one stimulating colour plate in this book (figure 138) is, for all its awkward composition, one which allows a heavy darkness and gloom as a legitimate part of the picture, as well as permitting a delightful Rackham excursion into the bizarre.

136 'New lamps for old', *Arthur Rackham's Fairy Book* 1933

137 'I at length found myself within view of the melancholy house of Usher'.
*Tales of Mystery and Imagination* 1935

Rackham's unhappiness with the direction in which his style was being cramped by his past—into what we might term 'visual or inspirational boredom' —is confirmed by a glance at the solutions he offered, once the problem was clearly formulated. He had two solutions, and there is evidence that he adopted both for a short while, but then succumbed to one only. He had a choice of moving into a new decorative and lyrical style, such as has been observed in *The Tempest*, or of returning to the pronounced formulas of his earlier work, and thereby giving up stylistic development. The style of work for a series of poems published by Harrap and Sons in the early thirties returned unashamedly to the early style. These books were *The Night Before Christmas* (1931), *Goblin Market* (1933) and *The Pied Piper of Hamelin* (1934).

Of the three *Before Christmas* is the least impressive, though each of the Christmas-card paintings has a vitality and charm which is lacking in many of

138 'Some of the wonders that you may now see', *Compleat Angler* 1931

139 'The children were nestled all snug in their beds', *The Night Before Christmas* 1931

the pictures produced by Rackham during that time. *Goblin Market*, which might easily have become an exercise in grotesqueries, has been infused with a delicacy of feeling and humour which touches the poem's own qualities very well, but here we have all the elements of early Rackham: beautiful women, goblins, anthropomorphized animals, black patches of grass illuminated by blobs of flowers (figure 140). *The Pied Piper* offers a pure Rackham theme of medieval houses, costumes and rhythms which served the artist well in his wish to return to the bawdy, hard, grotesque style which was so threatened by his emergent delicacy and lyricism—yet there is a flimsiness about these drawings which disappoints the Rackham-lover, and no doubt disappointed Rackham too.

A companion in format and style with the preceding three poems was *The King of the Golden River*, three plates of which fail completely to harmonize the disparate worlds of fantasy and realism, a failure which is virtually symbolized in the final plate (figure 142) which shows Gluck quite unrelated to the King of the Golden River, and neither related to the aqueous backcloth of clouds. With each of these plates of the Harrap series Rackham seems to have spent little time working out either composition or the underlying graphic possibilities within the illustration. The Rackham of *Rip van Winkle* is certainly under pressure at this time; whether the pressure be that of age or over-work, it is difficult to say.

According to Rackham, the illustrations he provided for Poe's *Tales of Mystery and Imagination*, in 1935, frightened even him, and whilst this might only be expected when a fine illustrator meets a fine and frightening text, it is in fact difficult to see precisely which of the drawings or paintings could instill fear. There is a fine admixture of quite pleasant Rackhams within the book, such as the plate showing Tripetta imploring for the threatened life of her friend, whilst the plate for 'Leonora' is in the Rackhamesque of *The Tempest*, and the picture of the Lady Ligeia, who 'came and departed as a shadow', is more a portrait of the large, old decaying city near the Rhine, than of any fearful thing, and in fact the cathedral spire looks somehow more insubstantial than Ligeia herself. The best plates are not so much frightening, as indicative of a grandeur and vision one might not so far have perceived in Rackham. The magnificent view of the melancholy house of Usher (figure 137) is of this order, the stunted Rackham trees being used not so much as an emotive source of fear or imagination, but as a grotesque and curvilinear foil to emphasize the linear solemnity

140  Frontispiece to *Goblin Market* 1933

141 'He would sit on a wet rock and fish all day',
*Rip van Winkle* 1905

of the house itself. One may list the plates which may be in any sense termed 'frightening' on the fingers of one hand. We find one fairly ordinary knifing ('The Gold Bug') such as may be found in any boy's comic book at least once a week; one very peaceful death ('The Oval Portrait'), which without the text might well be taken as a picture of a sleeping lady; a spectral image which is almost funny in its attempt to strike fear ('The Masque of the Red Death'), and in this same story we may feel constrained to ask if the colour plate of the masqueraders is meant to be fearsome or merely funny. There is a picture of a frightened man, which instils no fear in us, though with delicious Rackham borders which instil delight. It could be that in the charred remains of the king and privy councillors of Hop-Frog's last jest, some might find a sense of distaste or ill-ease; the descent into the maelstrom we may hardly identify with, since the human is too small within the huge current. One picture which seeks obviously to be quite gruesome is the one which shows the orang-utang, razor in one hand, severed scalp in another, but unfortunately there is a cartoon quality about the illustration (who can draw in line a monkey, without it appearing funny?) which removes it from the fulsome text: 'With one determined sweep of its muscular arm it nearly severed her head from her body. The sight of the blood inflamed its anger into frenzy. Gnashing its teeth, and flashing fire from its eyes, it flew upon the body of the girl, and imbedded its fearful talons in her throat, retaining its grasp until she expired.' Perhaps not a book or set of illustrations for a night's reading in bed, alone—but given the situation and the

164

need, I would prefer infinitely the pictures to the text, for at the best these amuse, at the worst merely raise graphic problems in the mind.

Ultimately the assessment of a set of illustrations must come down to personal taste, and in regard to Rackham there is no clearer indication of this crisis of taste than in the illustrations he provided for *Peer Gynt*—a nordic tale, yet one constructed in a warm climate*, in the same year that Rackham was born. Perhaps, because it is an epic (though it has been called many things: 'a poetic fantasy', an 'esoteric saga', even 'a satire') Rackham somehow fails to get near to its spirit of feeling. He is an illustrator more able to provide imagery for Dickens than for the epic of Ibsen. In the troll scenes, or in Peer's moorland encounter with the threadballs (figure 143), Rackhamerie abounds, but it is not in these scenes that the real grandeur of *Peer Gynt* is to be found. It was courageous of Rackham to tackle the death of Aase (peaceful death has rarely made a good subject for the graphic illustrator, being more the domain of literature because it is a sequential thing, rather than something which may be dealt with in an isolated cross-section of time), but the beautiful speech within the scene depends

*Written in southern Italy, and, as Ibsen delightfully said, 'So far away from one's future readers, one becomes rather reckless.'

142 'Before Gluck stood his old acquaintance, the King of the Golden River', *The King of the Golden River* 1932

143 'Peer and the Threadballs', *Peer Gynt* 1936

more on the visual effect of Peer sitting on the heaven-bound sleigh bed than
Rackham suggested. Again, whilst it is possible for soliloquy to suggest that the
statue of Memnon in Egypt reminds one of the Troll King, it is another thing for
an artist to so distort the appearance of this statue as to make it look more like
the Troll than the Memnon statue itself. The connexion between the two is an
important one to the theme, for it is the ancient statue which asks Peer where
the epic past of Norway is now (does it reside only in the subterranean palaces,
the racial subconscious of the nordic people?), but what is permissible for verbal
symbolism and allusion is not always permissible for the visual. As a result, the
contemplation of the Memnon statue, which might have been given a visually
epic quality, is one of Rackham's most unfortunate drawings (figure 144). So
distant from the real epic and esoteric feeling of the author, Rackham has
become merely insipid, even out of his depth, and while the illustrations within

166

144 'Peer and the statue of Memnon', *Peer Gynt* 1936

*Peer Gynt* may be considered reasonably proficient Rackhams, they are far away from the original text.

The final book published during Rackham's lifetime was the Limited Editions Club's *A Midsummer-Night's Dream* of 1939, which reproduced Rackham's work lithographically, from water-colours; a great pity, and a great failure, for it had always been the line from which Rackham's gothic fancy bred. The six colour plates are good, but in no way do they compare with the best of his earlier illustrations for the same title. His picture 'Enter Peaseblossom, Cobweb, Moth, and Mustard-seede' (figure 133) is a pastiche of an earlier plate (figure 145), yet even so it lacks conviction, perhaps because it lacks line.

145 'Enter Peaseblossom, Cobweb, Moth, and Mustardseed', *A Midsummer Night's Dream* 1908

*The Wind in the Willows* was not published in England until 1950, but it found two publishers, one for a de luxe edition (The Limited Editions Club, New York) and one for a trade edition (The Heritage Press, New York) in the United States posthumously in the year following Rackham's death. The book is a gentle delight, presenting sixteen illustrations which in no way fight with the more famous imaginative world created by Shepherd, although if Shepherd had not preceded him, then Rackham might have anthropomorphized his creatures even more. Several of the plates are delightful: the 'Golden Day when the three heroes walked by the Caravan, Mole leading a happy horse'; the placid Rat handing a hamper to put into a boat (figure 147), a plate famous among Rackham-lovers because it was the boat for which Rackham forgot to draw the oars, an

146 'It was a golden afternoon. The smell of the dust they kicked up was rich and satisfying', *The Wind in the Willows* 1940

omission which some see as significant in view of the artist's imminent death. Perhaps the most interesting picture is the frontispiece, which depicts the egocentric Toad levelled to the drab clothes of a no-pocket washerwoman, hopping about permissively, totally unequipped for the real contest. In the real world of people, like all egoists, animal or human, he is alien, and it is a typical piece of Rackhamerie that we should see two children laughing at the glum toad, not because he is a toad, but because he is obviously pretending to be something else.

It is with a sense of a serious loss that one turns to the imprint of the de luxe edition in search of the familiar Rackham signature, and finds not the careful hand of Rackham, but that of the designer Bruce Rogers, who saw the book and Rackham's pictures through the press.

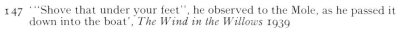

147 '"Shove that under your feet", he observed to the Mole, as he passed it down into the boat', *The Wind in the Willows* 1939

# APPENDIX A

## Bibliography of first editions for which Rackham provided illustrations

An American correspondent writing to Rackham from Cleveland, Ohio, in some state of exhilaration because he had found two editions of a Rackham book not hitherto represented in his collection, tempers his description of his finds with the reflection that Rackham may well not be interested in them, 'since you do not seem to be a collector of your own works'. The fact is that Arthur Rackham, the one person in England who might easily have established a comprehensive collection of his books, appears to have had no strong wish to do so. He went to great lengths to help bibliographers during his lifetime, and some of his pencilled notes have helped in the construction of the present bibliographic list, but in general he showed little interest in preserving all the works in which his illustrations appeared. Inevitably, therefore, the collection of books inherited by his daughter Barbara, and augmented by her, while it contains the greater part of the more famous titles and the de luxe editions, and is distinguished by the flyleaf drawings and dedications in the hand of the artist, may in no way be described as complete. Although several private collectors in England boast complete sets of the de luxe editions, or even of all post-1905 titles, it is unlikely that there exists in England a complete Rackham library which includes all the titles listed in the following bibliography.

Through a series of purchases and bequests the finest public library collections of Rackham's printed work are those housed in the University collections of Texas at Austin, at Columbia University, and in the Free Library of Philadelphia. The British Library collection in London is short of many book titles, though between the British Library and the Newspaper Library at Colindale there is a fully representative collection of Rackham's early magazine work. The catalogues of the Victoria and Albert Museum, in London, show surprisingly few more titles than one might reasonably expect on the shelves of an average collector. It is therefore to the United States that one must turn for a comprehensive survey of Rackham's published work.

The important collection at Austin has been established mainly through the acquisition of the private collections of Alfred A. Knopf, William H. Koester, George L. Lazarus and Edward A. Parsons.* The Lazarus collection alone, which includes almost every known book containing illustrations by Rackham, consists of some 165 volumes, numerous periodicals, over two dozen ephemeral pieces, as well as many examples of his commercial designs. Many of the books from the Lazarus collection have Rackham's original water-colours on the front flyleaf, which makes them quite unique. The Parsons and Knopf collection consists mainly of the large-paper limited de luxe editions, many of which are in any case duplicated in the Lazarus collection.

*I am indebted for the information in this paragraph to the article by Jennifer Phillips, 'The Arthur Rackham Collection' in the Austin University of Texas *Library Chronicle*, 1971–72.

# APPENDIX A

Columbia University is indebted to Mr and Mrs A. C. Berol for the larger part of their Rackham collection, which at one time formed Sarah B. Latimore's collection, upon which the early bibliography of Rackman's work was constructed.

In the Free Library of Philadelphia is an important and fairly comprehensive collection of Rackham's books which was originally established by Grace C. Haskell, the co-author with Latimore of the early Rackham bibliography.

In the absence of similar easily available collections in public libraries in England, it is to these important American collections that I am indebted for much of the information contained in the following bibliography of first editions, and I would like in particular to thank the librarians at the University of Texas for information which has helped me to clarify a few points.

There have been so many reprints, new impressions and revised editions of titles illustrated by Rackham that a comprehensive bibliography would be bulky, complicated for the general reader, and fairly soon rendered out of date by later editions. The truth of this may be adduced from the publisher's note included in a new edition of *Rip van Winkle* as early as 1916: 'Complete Edition, with 51 Illustrations in Colour. First published (15s. net) September 1905. New impressions January 1907; August 1908; May 1909; November 1910. Cheaper Issue, with 24 Illustrations in Colour and many new Illustrations in the Text, October 1916.' Allied to this complexity, there is the fact that some of the so-called reprints have not always been made from the original artwork, with the result that many plates bear little relationship to those passed by Rackham (who was notoriously fussy in this matter) as suitable.

However, there is still a need for a simple bibliographic checklist, since all published bibliographies of Rackham to date (1975) are in some minor and even major respects inaccurate or incomplete. The following chronological checklist gives only first editions, reprints and new editions involving revised artwork, up to and including the final book illustrated by Rackham and published posthumously in 1940. The checklist includes books either entirely illustrated by Rackham, or titles to which Rackham willingly or unwillingly contributed drawings.

A useful author's alphabetic checklist on page 182 is cross-referred to this chronological list, which within a stipulated year is arranged alphabetically by author's surname. The abbreviations for the information setting out numbers of illustrations and so on are explained on page 172 below.

Information given within this checklist includes *date* of earliest known publication of title; the full name of the *author*, or editor or signator of introduction (in those rare cases where the title is published anonymously, then it is listed within this checklist under the name of the most significant contributor within the text); the full *title* of the book, as given on the title page; the *publishers* (or in rare cases where there is no named publisher, the printer), with the English publisher named first, when co-editions with the United States were produced; the number of colour *reproductions*, line drawings and decorative items within the text. Finally, where applicable, there is the reference to *original source* of drawings which are in effect being reprinted in book form: this information is intended to complement the material set out in appendix B.

In the few cases in which the total of illustrations by Rackham is not listed, personal examination of the books has not been possible.

## Abbreviations used in bibliography

*B/W*    Black and white—this implies a different technique to pen—sometimes pencil or even litho being used.

*caps*    Decorative capital letters, drawn by Rackham.

*col.*    Full-colour, unless otherwise stipulated, as for example 2-col., which refers to two-colour illustration, prepared as separations.

*cont.*    Contributed by Rackham. This implies that other artists provided illustrations within the same text.

*ed.*    Edited by.

*e/p*    End-papers designed by Rackham.

*DL*    De luxe edition. In all cases, the de luxe edition (which sometimes contained an extra plate) was published alongside an ordinary or trade edition.

*f/p*    Frontispiece designed by Rackham.

*et al.*    And others. Stories produced by others than those named.

*intro.*    Introduced by, or introduction by.

*line*    Line illustrations. This includes all drawings other than tiny decorative items, and small vignettes, unless otherwise stipulated.

*LF*    'Little Folks'.

*p*    Page within the present text.

*photo.*    Photographic. A term used to describe a style of painting used by Rackham in some of his early books. See page 51.

*pos.*    Possibly. In a few cases it is not always possible to attribute with great certainty a drawing to Rackham.

*pseud.*    Pseudonym of.

*repeat*    Publishers frequently repeat one drawing (especially decorative motives and endpieces) once or twice within the same text.

*silh.*    Silhouette.

*vig.*    Vignettes. The term is used for both head and tail vignettes.

*wash*    Wash drawing, sometimes incorporating line.

*WB*    'Westminster Budget'.

*//*    Some or all drawings in this title appeared previously in book (title indicated by author or initials of magazine and date of publication).

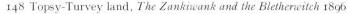

148 Topsy-Turvey land, *The Zankiwank and the Bletherwitch* 1896

# APPENDIX A

1893 Thomas Rhodes
*To the Other Side*
George Philip and Sons
(cont. 20 line)

1894 Annie Berlyn
*Sunrise-Land. Rambles in Eastern England*
Jarrold and Sons
(cont. 73 line)

1894 Fydell Edmund Garrett
*Isis Very Much Unveiled, Being the Story of the Great Mahatma Hoax*
'Westminster Gazette' Office
(cont. 1 line)

1894 Anthony Hope
*The Dolly Dialogues*
'Westminster Gazette' Office
(4 photo. wash)
Henry Holt & Co., New York
(1 photo. wash)

1894 Washington Irving
*The Sketch-Book of Geoffrey Crayon, Gent.*
G. P. Putnam's Sons (Holly Edition, New York and London)
(cont. 3 phot. wash)

1894 Lemmon Lingwood
*Jarrold's Guide to Wells-next-the-sea*
Jarrold and Sons
(cont. 51 line)

1895 Walter Calvert
*Souvenir of Sir Henry Irving*
Henry J. Drane, Chant & Co.
(cont. 2 wash, badly cropped) // WB

1895 William Ernest Henley
*A London Garland. Selected from Five Centuries of English Verse*
Macmillan & Co.
(cont. 1 line)

1895 Washington Irving
*Tales of a Traveller*
G. P. Putnam's Sons, London and New York
(cont. 5 photo. wash)

1895 Washington Irving

*The Sketch-Book of Geoffrey Crayon, Gent.*
G. P. Putnam's Sons (Van Tassel Edition, New York and London)
(cont. 4 photo. wash)

1895 'The Philistine' (pseud.)
*The New Fiction and other Papers*
'Westminster Gazette' Office
(1 line)

1895 Henry Charles Shelley
*The Homes and Haunts of Thomas Carlyle*
'Westminster Gazette' Office
(1 line, pos. others)

1896 Shafto Justin Adair Fitzgerald
*The Zankiwank and the Bletherwitch*
J. M. Dent & Co., London;
E. P. Dutton & Co., New York
(40 line)

1896 Hulda Friederichs
*In the Evening of his Days. A Study of Mr Gladstone in Retirement*
'Westminster Gazette' Office
(cont. 10 line) // WB

1896 Washington Irving
*Bracebridge Hall*
G. P. Putnam's Sons, London and New York
(cont. 5 photo. wash)

1896 Henry Seton Merriman
(pseud. Hugh Stowell Scott)
and S. G. Tallentyre
*The Money-Spinner and other Character Notes*
Smith, Elder & Co.
(12 photo. wash)

1897 Maggie Browne
(pseud. Margaret Hamer)
*Two Old Ladies, Two Foolish Fairies and a Tom Cat*
Cassell & Co.
(4 col. 19 line) // LF 1896—see p 35 above

1897 William Carlton Dawe
*Captain Castle. A Tale of the China Seas*

Smith, Elder & Co.
(f/p photo. wash)

1897 Thomas Tylston Greg
*Through a Glass Lightly*
J. M. Dent & Co.
(t/p pos. 2 vig.)

1897 Charles James Lever
*Charles O'Malley, The Irish
Dragoon*
Service & Paton, London; G. P.
Putnam's Sons, New York
(16 line)

1897 Henry Seton Merriman
(pseud. Hugh Stowell Scott)
*The Grey Lady*
Smith, Elder & Co.
(12 photo. wash)

1898 Frances Burney
*Evelina, or the History of a Young
Lady's Entrance into the World*
George Newnes
(16 line)

1898 Thomas Ingoldsby
(pseud. Richard Harris Barham)
*The Ingoldsby Legends: or Mirth
and Marvels, by Thomas Ingoldsby,
Esquire*
J. M. Dent & Co.
(12 col. 80 line, e/p)

1898 Stanley John Weyman
*The Castle Inn*
Smith, Elder & Co.
(f/p photo. wash)

1899 George Albemarle Bertie Dewar
*Wild Life in Hampshire Highlands*
Haddon Hall Library,
J. M. Dent & Co.
(19 line some repeats, e/p)

1899 Sir Edward Grey
*Fly Fishing*
Haddon Hall Library,
J. M. Dent & Co.
(cont. 19 line some repeats, e/p)
// Dewar '99

1899 Samuel Reynolds Hole
*Our Gardens*
Haddon Hall Library,

J. M. Dent & Co.
(cont. 26 line some repeats, e/p)
// Dewar '99

1899 Charles and Mary Lamb
*Tales from Shakespeare*
J. M. Dent & Co.
(f/p col. 11 line)

1899 Harriet Martineau
*Feats on the Fjord*
J. M. Dent & Co.
(f/p col. 11 line)

1899 Lady Rosalie Neish
*A World in a Garden*
J. M. Dent & Co.
(cont. 15 line some repeats)
// Dewar '99

1899 William James Tate
*East Coast Scenery*
Jarrold & Sons
(cont. 7 line)

1900 Country Life Library
(no named editor)
*Gardens Old and New (Vol. 1)*
Country Life Library
(cont. 9 decorative heads all
repeated)

1900 Jacob Ludwig Carl Grimm
and Wilhelm Carl Grimm
*Fairy Tales of the Brothers Grimm*
(trans. Mrs Edgar Lewis)
Freemantle & Co.
(f/p & title in col. 95 line, e/p)

1900 John Nisbet
*Forests and Woodlands*
Haddon Hall Library,
J. M. Dent & Co.
(cont. 11 line some repeats e/p)
// Dewar '99

1900 John Otho Paget
*Hunting*
Haddon Hall Library, J. M. Dent
& Co.
(19 line some repeats, e/p)
// Dewar '99

1900 Jonathan Swift
*Gulliver's Travels into Several
Remote Nations of the World*

J. M. Dent & Co.
(f/p col. 11 line)

1901 May Bowley [et al.]
*Queen Mab's Fairy Realm*
George Newnes
(cont. 5 line)

1901 Arthur George Frederick Griffiths
*Mysteries of Police and Crime*
(3 vols, final vol. 1902)
Cassell & Co.
(cont. 13 line) // Cassell's Mag. 1896

1901 Edwin Hodder
*The Life of a Century. 1800 to 1900*
George Newnes
(cont. 3 line 3 wash)

1901 Charles Richard Kenyon
*The Argonauts of the Amazon*
W & R Chambers
E. P. Dutton, New York
(6 photo. wash)

1901 Robert Henry Lyttelton
*Out-Door Games. Cricket and Golf*
Haddon Hall Library,
J. M. Dent & Co.
(cont. 12 line some repeats, e/p)
// Dewar '99

1901 Edmund Selous
*Bird Watching*
Haddon Hall Library,
J. M. Dent & Co.
(cont. 14 line some repeats, e/p)
// Dewar '99

1902 Horace Bleackley
*More Tales of the Stumps*
Ward, Lock & Co.
(cont. 9 line) // Cassell's Magazine
1901

1902 John Leyland (ed.)
*Gardens Old and New (Vol. 2)*
Country Life Library
(cont. 9 decorative heads all
repeated) // Vol. 1—1900

1902 Alexander Innes Shand
*Shooting*
Haddon Hall Library,
J. M. Dent & Co.
(13 line some repeats, e/p)

// Dewar '99

1903 Louisa Lilias Greene
*The Grey House on the Hill*
Thomas Nelson & Sons
(8 col. line by R. col. pos. by
another)

1903 George Alfred Henty
(*et al.*)
*Brains and Bravery*
W. R. Chambers
(8 photo. wash)

1903 Miranda Hill
*Cinderella*
*Little Folks* plays series.
Cassell & Co.
(2 col. 2 line)

1903 Barthold Georg Niebuhr
*The Greek Heroes*
Cassell & Co.
(4 col. 8 line)

1903 Marion Hill Spielmann
*Littledom Castle and other Tales*
George Routledge & Sons
(cont. 9 line) // LF 1902

1903 William Montgomery Tod
*Farming*
Haddon Hall Library, J. M. Dent
& Sons
(cont. 8 line) // Dewar 1899

1904 Maggie Browne
(pseud. Margaret Hamer)
*The Surprising Adventures of
Tuppy and Sue*
Cassell & Co.
(4 col. 19 line) // LF 1897

1904 Mary Cholmondeley
*Red Pottage*
George Newnes
(8 wash)

1904 Richard Henry Dana
*Two Years Before the Mast*
Collins' Clear-Type Press, London;
The John C. Winston Co., New
York
(8 col. line by R, dated 1902, col.
probably by another)

1904 William Price Drury
*The Peradventures of Private Pagett*
Chapman & Hall
(8 wash)

1904 Sam Hield Hamer
*The Little Folks Picture Album in
Colour*
Cassell & Co.
(cont. 1 col.) // LF 1899

1904 Henry Harbour
*Where Flies the Flag*
Collins Clear-Type Press
(6 col.)

1905 Washington Irving
*Rip van Winkle*
William Heinemann, London;
Doubleday, Page & Co., New York
(51 col. 3 line 1 init.) DL

1905 Sam Hield Hamer
*The Little Folks Fairy Book*
Cassell & Co.
(cont. 9 line) // LF various years

1905 Myra Hamilton
*Kingdoms Curious*
William Heinemann
(cont. 6 line) // LF 1905

1905 Arthur Lincoln Haydon
*Stories of King Arthur*
Cassell & Co.
(cont. 4 col. 2 line. Colour pos. by
another)
// LF 1902, original line

1905 Arthur Lincoln Haydon (*et al.*)
*Fairy Tales Old and New*
Cassell & Co.
(same as above *Stories of King
Arthur*, but bound up with four
other titles) // LF 1902

1905 Laurence Houseman
and W. Somerset Maugham (ed.)
*The Venture. An Annual of Art
and Literature*
John Baillie, London
(cont. 1 line)

1906 James Matthew Barrie
*Peter Pan in Kensington Gardens*
Hodder & Stoughton, London;
Charles Scribner's Sons, New York
(50 col. 3 line, e/p) DL

1906 Ralph Hall Caine (ed.)
*The Children's Hour: An Anthology*
George Newnes
(cont. 1 line)

1906 Rudyard Kipling
*Puck of Pook's Hill*
Doubleday, Page & Co., New York
(4 col.)

1907 Alfred E. Bonser, Emma Sophia
Buchheim and Bella Sidney Woolf
*The Land of Enchantment*
Cassell & Co.
(37 line) // LF 1896–1901. See
text p 185 below

1907 Lewis Carroll
(pseud. Charles Lutwidge Dodgson)
*Alice's Adventures in Wonderland*
William Heinemann, London;
Doubleday, Page & Co., New York
(13 col. 15 line, e/p) DL

1907 Eleanor Gates
*Good Night*
Thomas Y. Crowell Co., New York
(5 col.) // Scribner's Magazine,
1906

1907 Jacob Ludwig Carl Grimm
and Wilhelm Carl Grimm
*Fairy Tales of the Brothers Grimm*
(trans. Mrs Edgar Lucas)
Constable & Co., London;
Doubleday, Page & Co., New York
// Grimm 1900

1907 Thomas Ingoldsby
(pseud. Richard Harris Barham)
*The Ingoldsby Legends: or Mirth
and Marvels*
J. M. Dent & Co., London;
Doubleday, Page & Co.,
New York
(23 col. 77 line, e/p) // Ingoldsby
'98. DL

1907 J. Harry Savory
*Auld Acquaintance*

J. M. Dent & Co.
(cont. 2 line) //
Dewar, Fitzgerald, 1896

1907 J. Harry Savory
*Sporting Days*
J. M. Dent & Co.
(cont. 2 line) // Grey, 1899

1907 Pamela Tennant
*The Children and the Pictures*
William Heinemann
(1 line)

1908 Robert Burns
*The Cotter's Saturday Night*
J. Hewetson & Son, London
(f/p only)

1908 Bertram Waldron Matz (ed.)
*The Odd Volume. Literary and
Artistic*
Simpkin, Marshall, Hamilton,
Ken & Co.
(cont. 1 pen and pencil drawing)
// Ingoldsby 1898

1908 William Shakespeare
*Henry IV, Part II*
(Intr. A. Birrell)
Vol. xxiv of *The University Press
Shakespeare*
George G. Harrap & Co.
(f/p wash)

1908 William Shakespeare
*Macbeth*
(Intr. Henry C. Beeching)
Vol. xxxiii of *The University Press
Shakespeare*
George G. Harrap & Co.
(f/p wash) artwork dated 1903

1908 William Shakespeare
*A Midsummer-Night's Dream*
William Heinemann, London;
Doubleday, Page & Co., New York
(40 col. 34 line, e/p) DL

1909 De la Motte Fouqué
*Undine*
(adapted by W. L. Courtney)
William Heinemann, London;
Doubleday, Page & Co., New York
(15 col. 41 line, e/p) DL

1909 Jacob Ludwig Carl Grimm
and Wilhelm Carl Grimm
*Fairy Tales of the Brothers Grimm*
(trans. Mrs Edgar Lucas)
Constable & Co., London;
Doubleday, Page & Co., New York
(40 col. 62 line) // Grimm 1907,
but larger DL

1909 Charles and Mary Lamb
*Tales from Shakespeare*
J. M. Dent & Co., London;
E. P. Dutton & Co., New York
(12 col. 37 line some repeats, e/p)
// Lamb and Dewar, 1899 DL

1909 Mabel Hill Spielmann
*The Rainbow Book*
Chatto and Windus
(cont. 1 col. 15 line) // LF

1909 Jonathan Swift
*Gulliver's Travels into Several
Remote Nations of the World*
J. M. Dent & Co., London;
E. P. Dutton & Co., New York
(12 col. 34 line some repeats, e/p)
DL // Swift, 1899, and other Dent
publications

1910 Maggie Browne
(pseud. Margaret Hamer)
*The Book of Betty Barber*
Duckworth & Co.
(6 col. line by R, colour by another
12 line) // LF 1901. See text p 36

1910 Arthur Lincoln Haydon
*Stories of King Arthur*
Cassell & Co.
(cont. 4 col. 2 line. Colour
pos. by another) // LF 1902
original line

1910 Agnes Crozier Herbertson
*The Bee-Blowaways*
Cassell & Co.
(17 line with 2nd colour added)
// LF 1901

1910 Richard Wagner
*The Rheingold and the Valkyrie*
William Heinemann, London;
Doubleday, Page & Co., New York
(30 col. 8 line with repeats, e/p) DL

1911 Richard Wagner
*Siegfried and the Twilight of the
Gods*
William Heinemann, London;
Doubleday, Page & Co., New York
(30 col. 8 line with repeats, e/p) DL

1912 Aesop
(intr. G. K. Chesterton)
*Aesop's Fables*
William Heinemann, London;
Doubleday, Page & Co., New York
(13 col. 82 line t/p, e/p) DL

1912 James Matthew Barrie
*Peter Pan in Kensington Gardens*
Hodder & Stoughton, London;
Charles Scribner's Sons, New York
(50 col., 12 line, e/p)
// Mainly artwork for Barrie 1906,
with extra and reworked plates. DL

1912 Arthur Rackham
*The Peter Pan Portfolio*
Hodder & Stoughton; Brentano's,
New York
(12 col.) // Barrie 1906

1913 David Bearne
*Boy Ballads*
(I have been unable to find a copy of
this book listed by Hudson)

1913 Clifton Bingham *(et al.)*
*Faithful Friends. Pictures and
Stories for Little Folk*
Blackie & Son
(cont. 1 line) // LF

1913 Arthur Rackham
(intr. Sir Arthur Quiller-Couch)
*Arthur Rackham's Book of Pictures*
William Heinemann, London;
The Century Co., New York
(44 col. 11 line) DL // many sources:
see text above, and Appendix B,
page 183

1913 Arthur Rackham
*Mother Goose. The Old Nursery
Rhymes*
William Heinemann, London and
New York
(13 col. 78 line several vig. & caps,
e/p) DL // St Nicholas 1912–14

1914 Hall Caine (intr.)
*King Albert's Book*
'The Daily Telegraph'
(cont. 1 col)

1914 Julia Ellsworth Ford
*Imagina*
Duffield & Co., New York
(cont. 2 col.)

1914 Harriet Martineau
*Feats on the Fjord*
J. M. Dent & Sons
(8 col. line by R, colour by another)
// Martineau 1899

1915 Charles Dickens
*A Christmas Carol*
William Heinemann, London;
J. B. Lippincott Co., Philadelphia
(12 col. 17 line, e/p) DL

1915 John Galsworthy (Forward)
B. Harradey (text)
*The Queen's Gift Book*
Hodder & Stoughton
(cont. 1 col. 2 line)

1915 Lady Sybil Grant (*et al.*)
*Princess Mary's Gift Book*
Hodder & Stoughton
(cont. 1 col., 5 line)

1916 Edmund Gosse (intr.)
*The Allies' Fairy Book*
William Heinemann, London;
J. B. Lippincott Co., Philadelphia
(12 col. 23 line, e/p) DL

1916 Washington Irving
*Rip van Winkle*
William Heinemann, London;
Doubleday, Page & Co., New York
(24 col. 18 line 1 cap. t/p, e/p) DL
// Irving 1905

1917 Jacob Ludwig Carl Grimm
and Wilhelm Carl Grimm
*Little Brother and Little Sister*
Constable & Co., London; Dodd,
Mead & Co., New York
(13 col. 45 line, e/p) DL

## APPENDIX A

1917 Sir Thomas Malory
*The Romance of King Arthur and
his Knights of the Round Table*
(abridged by Alfred Pollard)
Macmillan & Co., London and
New York
(16 col. 16 line 54 decorative
blocks some repeats) DL

1918 Flora Annie Steel
*English Fairy Tales*
Macmillan & Co., London and
New York
(16 col. 43 line, e/p) DL

1918 Algernon Charles Swinburne
*The Springtide of Life. Poems of
Childhood*
William Heinemann, London;
J. B. Lippincott Co., Philadelphia
(8 col. 58 line, e/p)

1918 Francis James Child *(et al.)*
*Some British Ballads*
Constable & Co.
(16 col. 23 line)

1919 Julia Ellsworth Ford
*Snickety Nick and the Giant.
Rhymes by Witter Brynner*
Moffat, Yard & Co., New York
(3 col., 10 line)

1919 Charles S. Evans
*Cinderella*
William Heinemann, London;
J. B. Lippincott Co., Philadelphia
(1 col. 7 3-col. silh. 53 B/W silh.,
e/p) DL

1920 Charles S. Evans
*The Sleeping Beauty*
William Heinemann, London;
J. B. Lippincott Co., Philadelphia
(1 col. 8 3-col. silh. 57 B/W silh.
e/p) DL

1920 Jacob Ludwig Carl Grimm
and William Carl Grimm
*Snowdrop and Other Tales*
Constable & Co., London; E. P.
Dutton & Co., New York
(20 col., 29 line) // Grimm 1909

1920 Jacob Ludwig Carl Grimm
and Wilhelm Carl Grimm
*Hansel and Gretel and other Tales*
Constable & Co., London; E. P.
Dutton & Co., New York
(20 col., 28 line) // Grimm 1909

1920 James Stephens
*Irish Fairy Tales*
Macmillan & Co., London and
New York
(16 col. 20 line) DL

1921 John Milton
*Comus*
William Heinemann, London;
Doubleday, Page & Co., New York
(22 col. 35 line, e/p) DL

1921 Eden Phillpotts
*A Dish of Apples*
Hodder & Stoughton
(3 col., 26 line, e/p) DL

1922 Nathaniel Hawthorne
*A Wonder Book*
Hodder & Stoughton, London;
George H. Doran Co., New York
(16 col. 8 3-col. 21 line, e/p) DL

1923 Edmund Gosse (intr.)
*A Fairy Book*
Doubleday, Page & Co., New York
(11 col., 20 line)
// reprint, with fewer ill. of Gosse
1916

1923 L. Callender (ed.)
*The Windmill: Stories, Essays,
Poems and Pictures*
William Heinemann, London
(cont. 1 col.)

1924 A. C. Benson
and Sir Lawrence Weaver (ed.)
*The Book of the Queen's Dolls'
House*
Methuen & Co.
(1 small col. facsimile)

1925 Christopher Morley
*Where the Blue Begins*
William Heinemann, London;
Doubleday, Page & Co., New York
(4 col. 16 line, t/p, e/p) DL

1925 Ernest Rhys *(et al.)*
*The Book of the Titmarsh Club*
(printed by J. Davy & Sons)
(2 line, dated 1912 and 1909)

1925 Margery Williams
*Poor Cecco*
Chatto & Windus, London;
George H. Doran Co., New York
(7 col. 12 line some repeats) DL
// Good Housekeeping, 1925–26

1926 Erica Fay
*A Road to Fairyland*
G. P. Putnam's Sons
(cont. 1 col. f/p)

1926 William Shakespeare
*The Tempest*
William Heinemann, Ltd;
Doubleday, Page & Co., New York
(20 col. 20 line, t/p) DL

1927 Sir Robert Baden-Powell
*(et al.)*
*Now Then! A Volume of Fact,*
*Fiction and Pictures*
C. Arthur Pearson
(cont. 1 line)

1928 Abbie Farwell Brown
*The Lonesomest Doll*
Houghton Mifflin Co., Boston and
New York
(4 2-col., 26 line)

1928 Washington Irving
*The Legend of Sleepy Hollow*
George G. Harrap & Co., London;
David McKay Co., Philadelphia
(8 col. t/p & e/p 2 col. 32 line) DL

1928 Lewis Melville
(pseud. Lewis S. Benjamin)
*Not All the Truth*
Jarrolds
(cont. 1 line, dated 1909

1928 *A Birthday and Some Memories*
(I have been unable to
find a copy of
this book listed by Hudson)

1929 May Clarissa Byron
(prev. M. C. Gillington)
*J. M. Barrie's Peter Pan in*

*Kensington Gardens, Retold by*
*May Byron for Little People*
Hodder & Stoughton, London;
Charles Scribner's Sons, New York
(6 col. 16 line) // Barrie 1906 &
1912

1929 Oliver Goldsmith
*The Vicar of Wakefield*
George G. Harrap & Co., London;
David MacKay Co., Philadelphia
(12 col. 23 line, e/p) DL

1931 Charles Dickens
*The Chimes*
Limited Editions Club, New York
(19 line, f/p & t/p 2-col, e/p)

1931 Clement Clarke Moore
*The Night Before Christmas*
(originally an 1822 poem, 'A Visit
from St Nicholas')
George G. Harrap & Co., London;
J. B. Lippincott Co., Philadelphia
(4 col. 19 line, t/p, e/p) DL

1931 Izaak Walton
*The Compleat Angler*
(ed. Richard le Gallienne)
George G. Harrap & Co., London;
David McKay Co., Philadelphia
(12 col. 22 line, e/p) DL

1932 Lewis G. Fry (ed.)
*Oxted, Limpsfield and*
*Neighbourhood*
(printed: W & G Godwin)
(cont. 5 line)

1932 Hans Christian Andersen
(Note and selection by Rackham)
*Fairy Tales*
George G. Harrap & Co., London;
David McKay Co., Philadelphia
(12 col. 43 line 9 silh. e/p) DL

1932 John Ruskin
*The King of the Golden River*
George G. Harrap & Co., London;
J. B. Lippincott Co., Philadelphia
(4 col. 13 line, t/p 2-col., e/p) DL

1933 Arthur Rackham
*The Arthur Rackham Fairy Book*
George G. Harrap & Co., London;
J. B. Lippincott Co., Philadelphia

(8 col. 49 line 15 silh. e/p) DL
// a few repeats from earlier titles

1933 Christina Rossetti
*Goblin Market*
George G. Harrap & Co., London;
J. B. Lippincott Co., Philadelphia
(4 col. 19 line, e/p) DL

1933 Walter Starkie
*Raggle-Taggle. Adventures with a
Fiddle in Hungary and Roumania*
John Murray
(cont. 2 line)

1934 Robert Browning
*The Pied Piper of Hamelin*
George G. Harrap & Co., London;
J. B. Lippincott Co., Philadelphia
(4 col. 15 line 1 silh. e/p) DL

1934 Walter Carroll
*River and Rainbow. Ten Minatures
for Pianoforte*
Forsyth Brothers Ltd
(cover in B/W)

1934 Walter Starkie
*Spanish Raggle-Taggle. Adventures
with a Fiddle in North Spain*
John Murray
(cont. f/p & t/p)

1935 Julia Ellsworth Ford
*Snickerty nick. Rhymes by Whitter
Brynner*
Suttonhouse, Los Angeles &
San Francisco
(3 tone, 8 B/W) // Ford, 1919

1935 Edgar Allen Poe
*Tales of Mystery and Imagination*

George G. Harrap & Co., London;
J. B. Lippincott Co., Philadelphia
(12 col. 28 line, e/p) DL

1936 Henrik Ibsen
*Peer Gynt*
George G. Harrap & Co., London;
J. B. Lippincott Co., Philadelphia
(12 col. 38 line, e/p) DL

1936 Walter Starkie
*Don Gypsy*
John Murray
(cont. f/p & t/p)

1938 Percy Mackaye
*The Far Familiar*
Richards Press
(B/W f/p)

1938 Arthur Rackham
(no text)
*Costume through the Ages*
Maggs Bros
(6 line repros of colour originals)

1939 William Shakespeare
*A Midsummer-Night's Dream*
The Limited Editions Club, New
York
(6-col.—watercolours printed
lithographically)

1940 Kenneth Grahame
*The Wind in the Willows*
The Limited Editions Club, New
York; The Heritage Press, New
York
(not printed in England until 1950,
by Methuen)
(16 col. decoration on t/p) DL

## List of Authors

Aesop 1912
Albert 1914
Andersen H. C. 1932
Anonymous 1895, 1900, 1906
Baden-Powell R. 1927
Barham R. H. 1898, 1907
Barrie J. M. 1906, 1912
Bearne D. 1913
Benson A. C. 1924
Benjamin L. S. 1928
Berlyn A. 1894
Bingham C. 1913
Bleackley H. 1902
Bonser A. E. 1907
Bowley M. 1901
Brown A. F. 1928
Browne M. 1897, 1904, 1910
Browning R. 1934
Buchheim E. S. 1907
Burney F. 1897
Burns R. 1908
Byron M. C. 1929
Caine H. 1914
Caine R. H. 1906
Callender L. 1923
Calvert W. 1895
Carroll L. 1907
Carroll W. 1934
Chesterton G. K. 1912
Child F. J. 1919
Cholmondeley M. 1904
Country Life Library 1900, 1902
Courtney W. L. 1909
Crayon G. 1894, 1895
Dana R. H. 1904
Dawe W. C. 1897
Dewar G. A. B. 1899
Dickens C. 1915, 1931
Dodgson C. L. 1907
Drury W. R. 1904
Evans C. S. 1919, 1920
Fay E. 1926
Fitzgerald S. J. A. 1896
Ford J. E. 1914, 1919, 1935
Fouqué de la M. 1909
Friederichs H. 1896

Fry L. G. 1932
Gallienne R. le 1931
Galsworthy J. 1915
Garrett F. E. 1894
Gates E. 1907
Gillington M. C. 1929
Goldsmith O. 1929
Gosse E. 1916, 1923
Grahame K. 1940
Grant S. 1915
Greene L. L. 1903
Greg T. T. 1897
Grey E. 1899
Griffiths A. G. F. 1901–02
Grimm J. L. C. & W. C. 1900, 1907, 1909, 1917, 1920
Hamer M. 1897, 1904, 1910
Hamer S. H. 1904, 1905
Hamilton M. 1905
Harbour H. 1904
Harradey B. 1915
Hawthorne N. 1922
Haydon A. L. 1905
Henley W. E. 1895
Henty G. A. 1903
Herbertson A. C. 1910
Hill M. 1903
Hodder E. 1901
Hole S. R. 1899
Hope A. 1894
Housman L. 1905
Ibsen H. 1936
Ingoldsby T. 1898, 1907
Irving W. 1894, 1895, 1896, 1905, 1916, 1928
Kenyon C. R. 1901
Kipling R. 1906
Lamb C. and M. 1899, 1909
Lever C. J. 1897
Leyland J. 1902
Lingwood L. 1894
Lucas E. 1907
Lyttleton R. H. 1901
Mackaye P. 1938
Maggs 1938
Malory T. 1917
Martineau H. 1899, 1914

Mary, Princess 1915
Matz B. W. 1908
Maugham W. S. 1905
Melville L. 1928
Merriman H. S. 1896, 1897
Milton J. 1921
Moore C. C. 1931
Morley C. 1925
Neish R. 1899
Niebuhr B. G. 1903
Nisbet J. 1900
Paget J. O. 1900
'Philistine' 1895
Phillpotts E. 1921
Poe E. A. 1935
Pollard A. 1917
Queen 1915
Quiller-Couch A. 1913
Rackham A. 1912, 1913, 1932, 1933, 1938
Rhodes T. 1893
Rhys E. 1925
Rossetti C. 1933
Ruskin J. 1932
Savory J. H. 1907
Scott H. S. 1896, 1897
Selous E. 1901
Shakespeare W. 1908, 1926, 1939
Shand A. I. 1902
Shelley H. C. 1895
Spielmann M. H. 1903, 1909
Starkie W. 1933, 1934, 1936
Steel F. A. 1918
Stephens J. 1920
Swift J. 1900, 1909
Swinburne A. C. 1918
Tallentyre S. G. 1896
Tate W. J. 1899
Tennant P. 1907
Tod W. M. 1903
Wagner R. 1910, 1911
Walton I. 1931
Weaver L. 1924
Weyman S. J. 1898
Williams M. 1925
Woolf B. S. 1907

# APPENDIX B

## Rackham's early magazine illustrations which appeared in later books

Rackham's early drawings for newspapers and periodicals have never been adequately catalogued, even though many of these contained some of his finest work, and were often used in book titles which helped to establish his reputation. The checklist of periodicals provided by Bertram Rota in Derek Hudson's work on Rackham contains errors and omissions. It appears that Bertram Rota prior to 1960, in the first edition, and Anthony Rota, in the second edition of Hudson's work, in 1973, followed an earlier bibliographic checklist by Latimore and Haskell (Sarah Briggs Latimore and Grace Clark Haskell, *Arthur Rackham: a bibliography*, Los Angeles, 1936), just a little too faithfully, and without reference to the actual magazines which they listed. For example, both groups of bibliographers miss the May and November illustrations for *St Nicholas*, for the year 1913, whilst they give the remaining eight issues in which Rackham's pictures appeared during that year. The omission began with Latimore and Haskell. The similar mistakes and many omissions in the listing of work for *Little Folks* and for *Cassell's Magazine* are even more erratic and both lists are quite unreliable.

For this reason I have considered it advisable to construct a separate appendix listing the works which appear in the more important of the early magazines named. Since these periodicals play an important part in the establishing of Rackham's reputation, I have also indicated the titles of the books in which the illustrations were used, where this is appropriate.

The reference to book titles is by author and date, and these may be used to check for further information against the bibliography of books illustrated by Rackham on page 170 of this present work.

## Cassell's Magazine

1896 Feb. Arthur Griffiths
'Recent Escapes from Gaol'
(5 line)
Some used in Griffiths 1901

Mar. Anonymous
'The Gatherer'
(2 line)

Apr. Arthur Griffiths
'Unsolved Mysteries of Crime'
(6 line)
Some used in Griffiths 1901

Dec. Roma White
'The Dream Picture'
(4 line)

1897 Feb. J. Ashton
'History and Romance of Hyde
Park'
(1 line)

Jun. Alfred T. Story
'Sixty Years Ago and Now'
(13 line)

1898 Mar. Anonymous
'Told in Ashes'
(11 line)

Mar. F. M. Holmes
'The Story of the New River
Company'
(cont. 1 line)

Jul. Myra Hamilton
'The Doll's Romance'
(2 line)

1899 Jul. C. V. Godby
'At Henley'
(1 line)

Sep. C. V. Godby
'The Red Fiend'
(12 line in border)

1900 Dec. C. V. Godby
'Stage-Land'
(several line drawings around text
on double-page spread)

1901 Feb. M. Randal Roberts
'The Oddest Contests Record'
(5 line)

Jun. Horace Bleackley
'A Clerical Error'
(2 line)
Used in Bleackley 1902

Aug. Horace Bleackley
'The Magic Bat'
(4 line)
Some used in Bleackley 1902

Sep. Horace Bleackley
'In the Days of Top-Hats'
(5 line)
Some used in Bleackley 1902

Oct. Henry A. Hering
'Two Professors and One Mummy'
(3 line)

1902 Mar. C. V. Godby
'Tit for Tat'
(8 line drawings in border around
text)

May C. V. Godby
'New Noses for Old Ones'
(7 line drawings in border around
text)

Dec. C. V. Godby
'To My Stocking'
(6 line drawings in border around
text)

Dec. B. Fletcher Robinson
'Ghosts and Their Funny Ways'
(8 line)

1903 Feb. Halliwell Sutcliffe
'Nick O' Desperates'
(1 line)

Mar. Fox Russell
'The Sorrows of an Amateur Actor'
(2 line)

Mar. F. M. Holmes
'Remarkable Beds'
(cont. 2 line)

Dec. C. V. Godby
'Old Friend Christmas'
(7 line drawings in border around
text)

# Little Folks

1896 Feb. 'Simple Simon'
'The Songs of Simple Simon'
(2 line)

Mar.–Apr. A. E. Bonser
'The Maker of Ghosts and the
Maker of Shadows'
(3 line in each of two articles)
Used in Bonser 1907

Apr. 'Simple Simon'
'The Songs of Simple Simon'
(2 line)

Jul.–Dec. Maggie Browne
'The Surprising Adventures of
Tuppy and Sue'
(4 line for three months, 3 line for
three months)
Used in Browne, 1897

Jul.–Aug. A. E. Bonser
'The Mines of Experience'
(3 line in both months)
Used in Bonser, 1907

1897 Jan. Anonymous
'The Little Folks Entertainment
Album'
(A give-away booklet inserted in
LF, with *possibly* 3 line drawings
by Rackham)

Jan.–Jun. M. E. Hobson
'The Narrations of Peter Troll,
Elf: or, Dips into Foreign Folk
Lore'
(1 line in each of six parts)

Jul.
Editorial vignette for 'Little Folks'
repeated many time in
subsequent issues

Jul.–Dec. Philip Gibbs
'The Adventures of an Arch-
Rogue'
(1 illustration in 2-colour, for each
of six parts)

Sep. A. E. Bonser
'The Terrible Trouble of Forty
Winks'
(1 line)

1897 Nov.–Dec. Anonymous
'Cinderella. A Play in Three
Scenes'
(2 line illustrations in 2 colours for
each of two parts)

1898 Jul.–Dec. M. B. Hobson
'Barbara's Flame Fairy'
(1 line illustration in 2 colours for
each of six parts)

Nov.–Dec. Anonymous
'Boy or Girl'
(1 line illustration in 2 colours for
each of two parts)

1899 Jan.–Jun. Kathleen Kerr
'Rama. An Indian Legend'
(1 line in each of six parts)

Jul. Arthur Rackham
'Up a Tree'
(1 colour plate by Rackham)
Used in Hamer, 1904

Jul. Anonymous
'Pretty Pictures to Paint'
(a give-away booklet inserted in
LF, to which Rackham contributed
1 illustration in 2-colours, and the
same without colour)

Jul.–Dec. A. E. Bonser
'The Stories of Ben the Sailorman'
(2 line for each of 5 parts, with
1 line only for Oct. issue)
Used in Bonser, 1907

1900 Jan.–Jun. Harold Avery
'The House by the Moor'
(4 line Jan., 3 line for next 4
months, and 4 line for June)

1900 Jul.–Dec. Bella Sidney Woolf
'Harry and Herodotus'
(1 line in B/W, with 2-colour
roller overlay, in each of 6 parts)
Used (line only) in Bonser, 1907

1901 Jan.–Jun. Maggie Browne
'The Book of Betty Barber and
the Trouble it Caused'
(3 line in each of 6 parts)
Used in Browne, 1910

Jul.–Dec. E. S. Buchheim
'Stories from the Edda'
(1 line in B/W with 2-colour
roller overlay, in each of 6 parts)
Used (line only) in Bonser, 1907

1902 Jan–Jun. B. S. Woolf
'Harry and Herodotus'
(1 line in B/W, with 2-colour
roller overlay, in each of six parts)
Used (line only) in Bonser, 1907

Jul.–Dec. A. L. Haydon
'Stories of the Table Round'
(1 line in each of 6 parts)
Used in Haydon, 1905 and 1910

Jul.–Aug. M. N. Speilmann
'Littledom Castle'
(5 line in July, 6 line in Aug.)
Used in Spielmann, 1903

1903 Jan.–Jun. Myra Hamilton
'Arkel and the Princess Sakata'
(1 line in each of 6 parts)

Jul.–Dec. A. Lincoln
'Boys of Long Ago'
(1 line in each of 6 parts)

1904 Jul.–Dec. Wood Smith

'In the Land of the Mikado'
(1 line in each of 6 parts)

1905 Jan.–Apr. M. H. Spielmann
'Adventures in Wizard Land'
(3 line in each of four parts)
Used in Spielmann, 1909

Jan.–Jun. Myra Hamilton
'Big Town Little Town'
(1 line in each of 6 parts)
Used in Hamilton, 1905

Jul.–Dec. Myra Hamilton
'The Princess Banza'
(1 line in each of 6 parts)

Dec. Anonymous
'The Lost Crown'
(1 wash drawing)

1906 Jan. M. H. Speilmann
'Father Christmas at Home'
(3 line)
Used in Spielmann, 1909

1907 Oct. Anonymous
'Diamond Cut Diamond'
(1 pencil or crayon drawing)
Used in Rackham (Book of
Pictures), 1913, and in *St Nicholas*,
April, 1914

## St Nicholas

1898 Jul. A. E. Bonser
'The Treasure at the end
of the Rainbow'
(5 line)

1912 Dec. Rackham
'Mother Goose' series
(1 colour—'Ring a Ring O' Roses',
4 line)
Used in *Mother Goose*, 1913

1913 Jan. Rackham
'Mother Goose' series
(2 colour—'The Man in the
Wilderness' and 'Little Miss
Muffet', 3 line)
Used in *Mother Goose*, 1913

1913 Apr. Rackham
'Mother Goose' series
(1 colour—'Jack and Jill', 1 line)
Used in *Mother Goose*, 1913

1913 May Rackham
'Mother Goose' series
(1 colour—'The fair maid who the
first of May', 1 line)
*Used in Mother Goose*, 1913

1913 Jun. Rackham
'Mother Goose' series
(1 colour—'As I was going to
St Ives', 1 line)
Used in *Mother Goose*, 1913

1913 Jul. Rackham
'Mother Goose' series
(1 colour—'There was an old
woman lived under a hill')

1913 Aug. Rackham
'Mother Goose' series
(1 line—'Little Bo Peep')
Used in *Mother Goose*, 1913

1913 Sep. Rackham
'Mother Goose' series
(5 line)
Used in *Mother Goose*, 1913

1913 Oct. Rackham
'Mother Goose' series
(1 colour—'Hey! Diddle, Diddle,
the Cat and the Fiddle', 5 line)
Used in *Mother Goose*, 1913

1913 Nov. Rackham
'Mother Goose' series
(1 colour—'Bye, baby bunting',
5 line)
Used in *Mother Goose*, 1913

1913 Dec. Rackham
'Mother Goose' series
(2 colour—'Hark, Hark, the dogs
do bark' and 'Rain, Rain, go
away', 6 line)
Used in *Mother Goose*, 1913

1914 Jan. Rackham
'Mother Goose' series
(2 colour—'Mother Goose' and
'Jack Sprat and his wife', 5 line)
Used in *Mother Goose*, 1913

1914 Feb. Rackham
(1 colour—'The Magic Cup')
Used in *Arthur Rackham's Book of
Pictures*, 1913

1914 Mar. Eleanor Farjeon
'Arthur Rackham: The Wizard at
Home'
(1 colour—'Children in Kensington
Gardens, London', 5 line, 2 photos
of R's Hampstead House, 1 photo
of R's daughter)

1914 Apr. Rackham
(1 colour—'The Gossips')
The pencil or crayon drawing for
this appeared in *Little Folks*, Oct,
1907 and in *Rackham's Book of
Pictures*, 1913

1914 May Rackham
(1 colour—'Wee Folk')
Used in *Rackham's Book of
Pictures*, 1913

1914 Jun. Rackham
(1 colour—'The Frog Prince')
Used in *Rackham's Book of
Pictures*, 1913

1914 Jul. Rackham
(1 colour—'Marjorie and
Margaret')
Used in *Rackham's Book of
Pictures*, 1913

1914 Aug. Rackham
(1 line—'Jack and the Beanstalk')
Used in colour in *Rackham's Book
of Pictures*, 1913

1914 Oct. Rackham
(1 colour—'Puss in Boots')
Used in *Rackham's Book of
Pictures*, 1913

1914 Nov. Rackham
(1 colour—'Elves')
Used in *Rackham's Book of
Pictures*, 1913

1914 Dec. Rackham
(1 colour—'The Little People's
Market')
Used in *Rackham's Book of
Pictures*, 1913

1915 Jan. Rackham
(1 colour—'Hi! You up there!'
Used in *Rackham's Book of
Pictures*, 1913

# APPENDIX C

## The AR monogram on the illustrations to *A Dog's Mission* and *The Ferryman's Boy*
### (See page 29 above.)

To the observations set out on page 30, I would like to add the following points. The problem of the AR or the AJR monogram is a little more complex than most bibliographers (who are rarely art historians) appear to have realized.

The books were published in 1887 (but see footnote on page 29 above) and a survey of the 1887 volume of *The Year's Art* shows that according to the Directory of Artists for the relevant year, there are no fewer than thirteen artists who might legitimately have used one or other of these monograms. It may rightly be claimed that some of these individuals might well have been painters, rather than illustrators, but my point is that a monogram AR or AJR need not refer to Rackham exclusively.

From 1888 onwards, the Directory of this same useful annual admits the existence of one A. Rackham, who is recorded as living at 3 St Anne's Park Villas (later changed to 5 St. Anne's Park Road), Wandsworth in London, and thereafter for several years at a variety of different addresses in the London area. This is our A. Rackham. The Directory for 1890 gives not only this same A. Rackham of Wandsworth, but also Arthur Rackham of 11 Buckingham Street, The Strand, which is Rackham's address until his marriage. Curiously enough, whilst the Rackham of Wandsworth remains in these Directories of *The Year's Art*, the nominal *doppelganger* disappears after this one fleeting entry. The point is that Rackham did regard himself as an artist worthy of inclusion in the Directory a short time after publication of *A Dog's Mission*.

As for the monogram itself, a glance through the AR entries in Goldstein's *Monogram Lexicon* will convince anyone of the futility of arguing dubious provenance or title purely from the existence of an engraved monogram, for over ten artists used precisely such a range of monograms as may be confused with those used by Rackham in his early years. Indeed, there is one blockmaker and at least one other artist working contemporaneously with Rackham (and even within the same papers) prior to 1895, signing themselves with an AR.

If the above points are not sufficient to dispel the idea that Rackham may have drawn these unpleasant illustrations, it is worth observing that they do not resemble his early styles of drawing, nor do the monograms on them in any way resemble the four different monograms first used by Rackham in his earliest known published drawings.

# APPENDIX D

## The errors in Martin Hardie's *Water-colour Painting in Britain* (Vol III *The Victorian Period*) in so far as they touch upon Arthur Rackham

Since *Water-colour Painting in Britain* is a book frequently used by art students in their researches, it is worth pointing out the errors in the entry under Arthur Rackham on page 147 of the third volume. From the first paragraph dealing with Rackham: (i) Rackham was *not* educated at the Slade School; (ii) Shannon was not a fellow student; (iii) there is no evidence that either Ricketts or Shannon helped to interest Rackham in books; (iv) 'After some years of freelance work in black and white illustration' misstates Rackham's experience prior to his success; (v) Rackham did *not* first blossom into fame with his illustrations to *A Midsummer Night's Dream* of 1908; (vi) it is highly dubious to say that 'His work tended always to the sublime, never to the macabre', and one wonders which of Rackham's books he had in mind; (vii) Rackham did not illustrate merely over thirty books between 1905 and his death, but about ninety titles.

Hardie's appraisal of Rackham's technique in his second paragraph appears to be based upon an article by A. S. Hartrick, which does not go deeply into Rackham's widely versatile style. The third paragraph of Hardie's study contains further questionable propositions, the most important of which is the pronouncement that Rackham's success as a water-colour painter began with an exhibition of the original water-colours for *Rip van Winkle* at the Leicester Galleries in 1905. These were scarcely water-colours in the accepted sense of the word, but quite clearly illustrations—in any case, Rackham was already an Associate of the Royal Water-Colour Society as early as 1902, and well known as a painter in this genre.

# APPENDIX E

## Rackham's original drawings and paintings in public collections

The greater part of Rackham's original paintings and drawings has found its way into public and University collections in the United States of America. The largest collection, which includes many of the original sketchbooks, as well as water-colours and line drawings, is in the Butler Library at Columbia University, whilst the Free Library of Philadelphia, and the Public Library in New York (the Spencer Collection) houses many originals. The important collection in the University of Texas at Austin also incorporates original Rackhams, some of which have never been reproduced.

By this showing, the collection of original Rackhams in public and University collections in England is rather pathetic: the British Museum holds three, the Victoria and Albert 21, and the Tate Gallery only one. Odd drawings and paintings are scattered in the provinces, in Beverley, Bradford, Harrogate and Nottingham Art Galleries, in Cambridge (Fitzwilliam Museum), Preston (Harris Museum and Art Gallery) and Shrewsbury (Shrewsbury School, the Moser Collection). There are, of course, works in various private collections in the British Isles, but these are too numerous to mention here, save for a brief reference to the collection of Mrs Barbara Edwards, Rackham's daughter, who kindly allowed me to examine relevant material, such as sketchbooks, as well as rare editions, and also consented to allow reproduction of the many works in copyright.

# SELECTED BIBLIOGRAPHY

Baldry A. L.    'Arthur Rackham: A Painter of Fantasies', *The Studio*, May, 1905
Blackburn H. G.    *The Art of Illustration*, 1894
Braugham R.    *The Centenary of Arthur Rackham's Birth*, 1967
Coykendall F.    *Arthur Rackham: A List of Books Illustrated by Him*, 1922
Gardner E. L.    *Fairies. The Cottingley Photographs and Their Sequel*, 1966
Garner J.    'The Wizardry of Arthur Rackham', *International Studio*, July 1923
Gwynn F. L.    *Sturge Moore and the Life of Art*, 1952
Hardie M.    *Water-Colour Painting in Britain*, 1968
Hartrick A. S.    *The Old Water-Colour Society's Club*, Vol. XVIII, 1940
Hudson D.    *Arthur Rackham. His Life and Work*, 1960
Latimore S. B. and Haskell G. C.    *Arthur Rackham: A Bibliography*, 1936
Layard G. S.    'The Colour of Christmas: Thirteen Christmas Colour-Books and Their Artists', *The Bookman*, December 1922.
Lewis C.    *Self Portrait. Letters and Journals of Charles Ricketts*, 1939
Lewis C. S.    *Surprised by Joy*, 1955
Osborne E. A.    'Some Earlier Illustrated Books of Arthur Rackham', *The Bookman*, December 1933
Philips J.    'The Arthur Rackham Collection', *Austin University of Texas Library Chronicle*, 1971–72
Rota B.    *The Printed Work of Arthur Rackham*, 1960

# INDEX

## Index of book titles and magazines illustrated by Rackham

Aesop's Fables   14, 41, 64, 82, 83
Alice's Adventures in Wonderland   61, 66, 73, 114–16, 119, 146
Allies Fairy Book, The   134, 149
Arthur Rackham's Book of Pictures   50, 57, 77, 96, 131–3, 148
Arthur Rackham's Fairy Book   155, 158–9

Brains and Bravery   102
British Ballads   13
Book of Betty Barber, The   36, 40, 62

Cassell's Magazine   32, 63, 65, 66, 81, 98
Chums   17
Cinderella   138
Compleat Angler, The   159, 161
Comus   121, 139, 140

Dish of Apples, A   139, 140, 141
Dolly Dialogues, The   31, 102–3
Dog's Mission, A   29, 30, 188

English Fairy Tales   93–4, 137

Fairy Tales of the Brothers Grimm   44, 81, 119, 127
Fairy Tales of Hans Andersen   154, 155
Feats on the Fjord   36
Fishing   95

Goblin Market   161–2, 163
Greek Heroes, The   133
Gulliver's Travels   89, 91

Hunting   95

Ingoldsby Legends, The   33, 115, 118
Irish Fairy Tales   143–46, 155

Jarrold's Guide to Wells-next-the-Sea   38

King Albert's Book   16
King of the Golden River, The   162, 165

Land of Enchantment, The   103, 105–6
Little Brother and Little Sister   135–7, 147
Little Folks   35–6, 38, 45–6, 55, 58, 66, 69, 73, 81, 101–7, 133–4

Midsummer Night's Dream, A   42, 49, 85, 109, 118–19, 122, 124–5, 156, 167
Mother Goose   15, 131–2

Night Before Christmas, The   161–2

Pall Mall Budget, The   19, 20, 22–4, 28–9
Peer Gynt   67–8, 165–7
Peradventures of Private Pagett, The   102
Peter Pan in Kensington Gardens   13, 43, 52, 54, 60, 79, 110–12, 114, 118, 146
Pied Piper of Hamelin, The   161–2
Poor Cecco   147
Punch Almanack   104

Queen Mab's Fairy Realm   108
Queen Mary's Gift Book   134

Rainbow Book, The   39, 59, 106–8, 133
Red Pottage   102
Rheingold and the Valkyrie   70, 74, 119–20
Rip van Winkle   35, 53, 56, 66, 68, 71, 72, 85–8, 91–4, 97–8, 102, 109, 112–14, 116, 147, 164
Romance of King Arthur   137

Scraps   19–20
Shooting   95
Siegfried and the Twilight of the Gods   70, 74–6, 127, 129–31
Sketchbook of Geoffrey Crayon   85, 102
Sleeping Beauty, The   138
Some British Ballads   13
Springtide of Life, The   137
Stories of King Arthur   103, 106
Sunrise Land   31, 38, 162

Tales from Shakespeare   95
Tales of a Traveller   102
Tales of Mystery and Imagination   66, 160, 163–5
Tempest, The   143, 146, 150–51, 153, 163
Titmarsh Club, The   23
To the Other Side   29–30
Two Old Ladies, Two Foolish Fairies and a Tom Cat   36–6, 65, 99–100, 103

Undine   119, 123, 125–7

Westminster Budget, The   19–21, 24–8
Wild Life in Hampshire   94–6
Wind in the Willows, The   88–9, 168–9
Wonder Book   141–2, 152, 155, 157

Zankiwank and Bletherwitch, The   66, 99–101, 172